DEALING WITH THE
TOUGH STUFF

HOW TO ACHIEVE RESULTS FROM KEY CONVERSATIONS

DARREN HILL, ALISON HILL & DR SEAN RICHARDSON

WILEY

This edition first published in 2016 by John Wiley & Sons Australia, Ltd
42 McDougall St, Milton Qld 4064
Office also in Melbourne

Typeset in 11/13 pt ITC Berkeley Oldstyle Std by Aptara, India

© Pragmatic Thinking Pty Ltd 2016

The moral rights of the authors have been asserted

National Library of Australia Cataloguing-in-Publication data:

Creator:	Darren Hill, author.
Title:	Dealing with the Tough Stuff: How to achieve results from key conversations / Darren Hill, Alison Hill and Dr Sean Richardson.
Edition:	2nd edition
ISBN:	9780730327004 (pbk.)
	9780730327011 (ebook)
Notes:	Includes index.
Subjects:	Communication in management—Handbooks, manuals, etc.
	Conversation—Handbooks, manuals, etc.
	Personnel management—Handbooks, manuals, etc.
	Employees–Rating of—Handbooks, manuals, etc.
	Self-actualization (Psychology)—Handbooks, manuals, etc.
Other Creators/ Contributors:	Hill, Alison C., author, Richardson, Sean, author.
Dewey Number:	658.3145

Cover design by Wiley

Internal and cover illustrations © Pragmatic Thinking Pty Ltd

by C.O.S. Printers Pte Ltd

10 9 8 7 6 5 4 3 2 1

Disclaimer
The material in this publication is of the nature of general comment only, and does not represent professional advice. It is not intended to provide specific guidance for particular circumstances and it should not be relied on as the basis for any decision to take action or not take action on any matter which it covers. Readers should obtain professional advice where appropriate, before making any such decision. To the maximum extent permitted by law, the authors and publisher disclaim all responsibility and liability to any person, arising directly or indirectly from any person taking or not taking action based on the information in this publication.

CONTENTS

PREFACE

It all started with a printer.

Sue used to send her printing to the printer but, rather than immediately picking it up, would leave it for a few minutes—sometimes hours. Not with any intent. She just got distracted. But before casting a stone for this heinous crime, admit it: we have all done it.

John didn't like having to sort out someone else's printing when fetching his own. Who does? So one day he decided enough was enough and put up a sign above the printer. The sign read:

PLEASE PICK UP YOUR PRINTING.

IT IS DISRESPECTFUL TO LEAVE IT

FOR OTHERS TO SORT OUT.

Of course, you know what happened next. Sue—who left her stuff in the printer—saw the sign as a direct attack on her and felt offended and humiliated. And she responded in kind. Sue's retaliation wasn't overt or loud, but in her mind she placed a black mark against everything and anything John said or did in the office.

It started with small things: expressing opinions contrary to John's at the team meeting and refusing to participate in projects or working groups that John was involved in.

John also changed his behaviour towards Sue. Responding to Sue's contrary behaviour, John made every attempt to point out flaws, mistakes or shortcomings in Sue's work to anyone in the office who would listen.

The relationship had quickly become adversarial — the battlelines had been drawn.

Fast forward four years.

The team that Sue and John belong to is in total disarray. There are now not one, but two longstanding grievance procedures in place. Turnover of the best staff has been high, and morale and productivity are at an all-time low. Chaos reigns supreme.

The dysfunction within the work team has resulted in several workers' compensation claims for psychosocial injury (that's a fancy term for stress leave), and the cost to the organisation of this dysfunctional team is now estimated to be more than one million dollars.

How did things go so wrong?

The better question is this: Who is responsible?

It's easy to start with the person who left their printing behind, or perhaps the blame could be directed at the person who put up the rather direct sign. But the cold, hard truth is that the responsibility for this whole mess lies with the manager of the section, who did not control the key conversations that needed to happen at the start.

Blowups occur. Interpersonal tensions happen. It's a fact of life when you put two or more people in the same vicinity. Whether it's a difference in values, beliefs, actions, expectations or what we like or dislike for lunch, we're all unique and have our own opinions, and at some point that difference is bound to manifest in a potential disagreement or conflict.

While Sue and John's example may seem dramatic at face value (one million dollars in lost productivity, let alone the personal costs involved), the reality is that this situation is all too common. You may have a similar story to tell.

Our workplaces and society have forgone the necessary direct conversations in favour of cotton wool and avoidance. We have created systems, procedures and policies that enable longstanding conflict to survive through layers of bureaucracy and hinder quick resolution through robust conversation. The cost of this approach is considerable on so many levels, and yet these costs can be minimised, mitigated and even eliminated by a manager who leads well in a time of crisis.

If leadership is measured on a continuum, at one end might be maligned leadership, where the people who work for you speak badly of you, and maliciously obstruct or even sabotage their own or your work efforts. It's not a great place to be.

The other, more desirable, end of the management continuum is aligned leadership, where the thoughts, attitudes and behaviours of the entire workgroup come into line with each other.

In essence, the gap between aligned leadership and maligned leadership boils down to two things:

- the decisions we make
- the actions we take.

In picking up this book, you have made a very good decision.

As for the actions you take — well, that's where you come in, and we are in your corner all the way.

Darren, Alison and Sean

March 2016

ABOUT THE AUTHORS

 **Darren Hill** is one of Australia's most in-demand strategists with a client book of Fortune 50 and ASX Top-20 companies. The culture-change programs Darren works on have been used in PepsiCo, McDonald's, Siemens, Suncorp Bank and the Australian Federal Government to name a few.

Darren is a best-selling author whose work has appeared regularly across the Fairfax Group (including the *Sydney Morning Herald* and *The Age*), News Limited (*The Daily Telegraph* and *The Courier-Mail*), Business Insider and Smart Company. He now writes exclusively for *BRW*, and has appeared on the 'Today' show and Sky's 'Business News'.

A behavioural scientist and Executive Director at Pragmatic Thinking (www.pragmaticthinking.com), Darren understands people like few others do. It is his intricate knowledge of people and culture that sees him not only delivering international keynote presentations at conferences but also designing, delivering and implementing complex, cross-layered multiyear culture-change programs inside organisations.

www.darrenhill.com.au

Alison Hill is a psychologist who frequently appears on Channel 9's 'Mornings' program, regularly has articles published with Business Chicks, and is highly sought after to assist individuals and teams transition through the 'tough stuff'.

Her work has found its way inside a few big businesses you may have heard of...PepsiCo, Sydney Water, BHP Billiton, Bond University, Griffith University and BlueCare, just to name a few.

Alison presents her unique and authentic message as a sought-after keynote speaker, engaging her audience with humour, practicality and real-world thinking.

Alison is a founder and director of the super-cool behaviour and motivation strategy company Pragmatic Thinking.

www.alisonhill.com.au

Dr Sean Richardson is a registered psychologist with a PhD in the psychology of excellence. He has a wealth of experience with elite sports teams, both as a high performance consultant and as a former world-class athlete. Sean has helped a number of professional sports teams go from middle of the pack to number one, and has delivered leading-edge, high-performance presentations and programs into the likes of Suncorp, Johnson & Johnson, Chrysler, ANZ, AMP and Mercedes.

A successful TEDx speaker, mentor to pro coaches and executive leaders, and facilitator for elite performing teams, Sean is known for his powerful messages on the mindsets of excellence, and delivers game-changing IP to individuals and organisations on the five sciences for building and delivering sustained high performance.

www.drseanr.com

ACKNOWLEDGEMENTS

So much has happened since the release of our first edition of *Dealing with the Tough Stuff*. There was the cracking of bottles of champagne when we were at the top of booksellers' charts and the feeling of joy at seeing our title in various languages, but most of all our biggest thrill has been the responses from readers on email, social media or in person who have said this book has been a game changer. So our first thank you truly belongs to you: the reader. Much gratitude.

Darren wants to thank his two co-authors, Alison and Sean. Alison, you're a gift to this world. Anyone who knows you also knows what an understatement that is. It's been an amazing ride and we've got plenty of gas in the tank to go further. Richo, mate, can't wait to see you, Kate and the kids grow their roots and flourish, and the corporate world to be shifted by your quality of thinking. It's world class.

Alison wants to express her deep gratitude to her best friend and husband, Darren. Seeing the corporate world embrace your expertise and thinking, and being changed by your ability to tackle the toughest of tough stuff head-on is an inspiration. It's only the beginning too. Thanks also to our beautiful children, Patrick and Kate, with whom some of the strategies in this book have worked exceptionally well! You are our future! Sean, your passion to step up and bring your best to any project is awesome. Hanging with you makes anything seem possible.

Sean wants to thank Darren and Alison. I just dig the readiness of both of you to jump into big projects with the confidence of knowing we will get there somehow—your integrity and work ethic are nothing short of inspiring. Thank you, Darren, for being an extraordinary partner in business, inviting me to join you and Alison on ventures so dear to you, and for being such a great mate. Alison, I believe you are a quiet driver of much of our progress on this collaborative work, all while being an amazing mum. Thank you for being you. I also want to thank my team, Kate, Charlotte and Sam: your love and support make things easy and give my life meaning.

Together we would like to give special mentions—in no particular order—to Rowdy McLean, Matt Church, Michael Henderson, Emma Isaacs, Peter Baines, Ross Lyon, Joe Roberts, Anthony Day, Linda Taylor, Kirsty Mitchell and Jo Robertson. You've all been such a source of inspiration to us in so many ways. Richard Harmer, again for your integrity and contribution to the rough stuff, thanks mate. Thanks to Tricia, Randall and the team at Churchill Education for your ongoing support. Jason Fox and Kim Lam: you have no idea how much your creative living inspires us to continue to make great work. Of course, Jen and Dougz at Jaxzyn Design for your counsel on cover and graphics, a huge thanks. We'll never forget Sandra Butcher and Anna Morgan, our earliest champions, and we thank you for letting us loose on your organisations and laying the foundation of the Tough Stuff. Lucy Raymond, again, you're so damn lovely! Even when we are ridiculously slack in getting back to you, you still know how to give us a dressing down, and you are so lovely. It's a skill! Thank you also to the professional team at John Wiley & Sons, who have not only been a joy to work with but have been a wonderful help in making this book a reality, and a special thanks to Sandra Balonyi, our editor, who was a delight to work with.

To all of you who are at the forefront of the tough conversations at work, thank you for having the courage and desire to want to tackle these situations. The world needs your leadership and we admire you for what you step up and do every single day.

It isn't the
MEANINGFUL CONVERSATIONS
in the
GOOD TIMES
that define a leader; it's the ability to have a
MEANINGFUL CONVERSATION
at the
WORST
of times.

INTRODUCTION

If you were to sit down and list all the tasks, skills and abilities of a leader of note, the ability to establish a meaningful conversation would have to be among the highest ranked responses.

Interestingly, though, it isn't the ability to have meaningful conversations in the good times that defines a leader; it's the ability to have a meaningful conversation at the worst of times. It's having the key conversations at key times that makes a leader truly worth following.

It is inevitable that as a leader or manager you will face conversations that are less than great. These are the conversations we simply label as the Tough Stuff. And the Tough Stuff is different for everyone. For some it is the underperformance discussion with an employee; for others it is the conversation with an excellent worker who has stepped over the line in one area. It could be the termination discussion, or it could be the first conversation with a new graduate who has messed up. It could be any one of a thousand scenarios, but the common denominator is this: all of these discussions are tough, some more than others.

Making a difference

It is a simple fact: the difference-makers in any organisation are its leaders and managers. Our job description at Pragmatic Thinking is an awesome one: to make a difference to these difference-makers. Our profession sees us leap out of bed in the morning, excited to start another day—we are so passionate about working with, educating and mentoring this highly influential group of hard-working people.

So what is the area we've spent the most time on, and where we've achieved the biggest results? Helping the difference-makers deal with the tough stuff.

The ability of the difference-makers to have an unenviable, yet completely necessary, conversation is at an all-time low. Most have been shockingly under-coached in what is undoubtedly one of the most important skills any leader must possess: the ability to handle a crisis.

So, if you're one of the difference-makers, a leader or manager in your place of work, there is good news. We're here to help. We believe the processes, actions and methods described in this book will fundamentally change how you deal with the tough stuff. They will make your life easier, and you will achieve better outcomes from your team as a result. Our expectations are high, and for good reason: the information in this book is reliable and valid because it has been delivered to thousands of difference-makers just like you.

The foundation for success

Between us, we've had more than five decades of witnessing various levels of dysfunction in the workplace and we've seen common and uncommon examples of conflict handled both well and very poorly.

We can assure you the strategies and approaches we present in this book work. In fact, we guarantee it 100 per cent. All the elements of the strategies are tried and tested via a better testing process than any statistical analytics program: they have been shown to be robust through good, old-fashioned practical application. People put into place these strategies and their ability to handle the tough stuff gets easier.

Our 100 per cent guarantee is taken off the table if you don't have one thing in place. The success of a workable outcome rests on one foundational principle: the belief that all people are good.

We're challenged every day in relation to this belief by reports in newspapers or on television, and occasionally we come across someone who confronts us with a set of behaviours that make us challenge that belief. But the good in others can often be hidden from view—both your view and their view. Our belief is unshakeable: as much as the sun comes up in the east and sets in the west, we know it to be true.

The moment we forget this principle is the moment our chance of a favourable outcome is extinguished. When positive regard leaves the building, so does hope.

And as you step towards greater confidence in being able to approach and handle tough situations, this is the first belief that you need to tap back into. It is your true north.

Difficult behaviours, not difficult people

There is a plethora of books and workshop programs that use the title and theme of dealing with difficult people. We would like to clearly and succinctly state the following: this is not a book about dealing with difficult people.

In fact, we take umbrage at the 'dealing with difficult people' title, let alone the contents of any educational material that carries it. Any program or resource that classifies and labels individuals into certain types of 'difficult' people is setting the reader up for failure. The moment you label someone as difficult is the moment you'll get that behaviour. This labelling mentality creates a powerful psychological frame that people filter their current circumstance through, and as a result they see only difficult types of people. It is a self-fulfilling prophecy.

So what we choose to focus on is an entirely different approach. It is this: there are no difficult people; there are only difficult behaviours.

And behaviours, even the really difficult ones, can be changed, as we will show you in this book.

Manipulating for good

There is a well-worn myth that says: 'You cannot change other people; only people can change themselves'. We refer to this as a myth because the reality is that we all influence and change each other's behaviours every single day. If we were to go for a walk up the street together we could show you how we change the behaviour of others simply by smiling and being friendly to the people we come across.

Being able to deal with tough situations more confidently will require you to adjust your own behaviour. Role modelling is the key first step in being able to reflect the behaviour you desire from others.

But we are also going to explore ways to adjust the behaviour of others. This may sound to you a lot like manipulation—and that's exactly what it is.

Before we proceed, though, it's important to be clear on what we mean by manipulation. The origin of the word 'manipulation' means 'to mould and shape with the hands' and, when you think about it, that's what we do with each other every day. You have no doubt already been doing it to people today. As you walked in to work, you smiled and greeted others; as you sat down at your desk and as you passed others in the tea room, you were manipulating them in certain ways. When you purchased this book, you undoubtedly had an effect on the shop assistant, and if you ordered it online, you effected change on others. For starters, we're smiling!

We shape each other's behaviour with our hands, our minds, our speech and our body language, among other things. And that's manipulation, but the term 'manipulation' has earned itself a bad rap socially.

The only difference between manipulation and influence is the intent behind them. Manipulation with good intent is a great thing.

If what we're aiming for is a better outcome for me and a better outcome for you, then the intent behind the process of moulding and shaping others is a good thing. It's when the intent is that others lose so that I can win that manipulation can go sour.

Ensuring that your intent is good and that you hold onto the first principle that all people are good means we can move away from the social definition of manipulation being something that is bad and towards a more accurate definition: that manipulation is the way that we shape and mould others' behaviours. As a manager or a leader, it's your role to influence and mould others: make sure you don't shy away from this incredible responsibility.

Upgrade your expectations

Tough situations weigh heavily on us, emotionally and physically. They can keep us awake at night, they consume our thoughts, they tap into a range of strong emotions (they can churn your stomach, and give you headaches or neck pain), and they can infect other relationships around you. Tough situations have a way of following you home from work and having an impact on things outside of work. They are insidious, and if left, or dealt with poorly, they can become insidious for a long time.

We believe you should have high expectations of what is in this book because we know that having the confidence and the skills to be able to handle the tough stuff better can dramatically improve your life. That's a grandiose claim, but it's our hope that this will be the outcome for you.

Regardless of what your expectations were when you picked up this book and started reading, upgrade them. Entertain the thought that there may be something that you read that will fundamentally change how you deal with the tough stuff. If this isn't your filter, you might just miss out on something life-changing.

Think of it this way: before you picked up this book your method or path for dealing with the tough stuff may have been heading in the direction shown in figure 1 (overleaf).

Figure 1: your current path

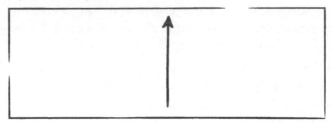

Let's say you learn something from reading these pages that just seems small today: just a little tip or a trick or a way to do things slightly differently, though it doesn't look that big in today's context (see figure 2).

Figure 2: your path after a small change in behaviour

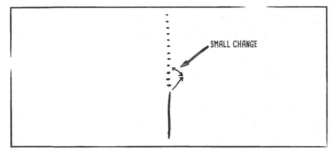

But you put the theory into practice and it works (we did tell you it works 100 per cent!) so you continue to use it (see figure 3).

Figure 3: small changes bring big results

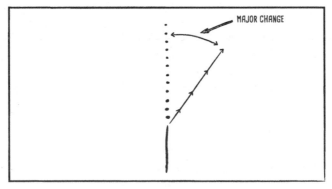

Then, over the course of that journey, over the following months or years, that small change could become huge.

Haven't you had a tough-stuff conversation where you have sat back and thought to yourself, 'I could have done that differently', and it weighed heavily on you for a while? A feeling of, 'If I could have changed this then the outcome would have been different'? Imagine if there were something in this book that allowed you to be able to influence a situation so that it did not escalate. Wouldn't that be a life changer?

Let's raise the bar on what these strategies could mean for you, because you have nothing to lose anyway. To quote from Michelangelo: 'The greatest danger for most of us is not that our aim is too high and we miss it, but that it is too low and we reach it'.

How to use this book

We are practical and pragmatic people, and that's how we want you to view and use this book. We have designed the book to provide you with a wealth of resources, information and portals to access ongoing learning.

The key to implementing changes is to start putting into place the strategies outlined in this book throughout your day-to-day activities. The strategies are purposefully practical and relevant for the workplace.

Here's another suggestion to assist you in maximising your learning throughout the book: whenever you come across a key point, practical strategy or new idea you want to use, note it down. Whether you use an electronic diary or a paper diary, take the time to add one note into your calendar every Monday morning for the next however-many weeks. If you make 25 notes while reading the book, you have just created six months' worth of Monday-morning reminders to help adjust and shape your behaviour.

Our insights

With a deep expertise in human behaviour (two psychologists, a behavioural scientist and all of us parents of very young children), we possess a wealth of understanding, experience and research in dealing with the tough stuff in our working careers. As well as providing you with key research, case studies and information, we have also provided you with our own insights from different points of view. At the end of each chapter you'll find insights from Darren, Alison and Sean, each from a slightly different perspective.

Darren's insights come from a behavioural economics perspective and relate the information in that chapter to the business environment. Darren loves the game of business.

Alison's insights consider the things that may get in the way of making changes and she suggests strategies for addressing these barriers by tapping into values, drivers and motivations.

As a former elite athlete, and now a consulting psychologist to some of North America's and Australia's highest profile sports and corporate organisations, Sean's insights will show you how you can relate key information to achieving success through high performance.

By bringing you our individual insights we aim to showcase other facets of human behaviour and interactions. Through our insights, we trust you will have your own insights along the way.

Stepping up to the challenge

Tackling the tough stuff in your workplace takes courage. It may not be the sort of courage that comes to mind when you think of someone skydiving or someone who runs through a burning house to save a small child. But it takes the everyday, ordinary courage of deliberate action. It takes the courage to stop avoiding situations: to say 'enough is enough', and to step up and be accountable.

By picking up this book, by choosing to make differences in how you deal with tough situations, by tapping back into your belief that all people are good, you are taking the courageous first step on a journey worth travelling.

1

WHAT'S YOUR TOUGH STUFF?

Getting clear on what's tough for you

Leadership can be a lonely place at times. Sure, there are few experiences more enjoyable than leading people towards great outcomes for both themselves and your organisation, but then there's the other side of leadership. There are the times when you won't see eye to eye with others. Conflict is inevitable. That's when the loneliness of leadership truly presents itself. It certainly is a tough gig being responsible for dealing with the tough stuff.

It's worth taking the time to be clear on what the tough stuff is for you: those key work conversations that you have to have and that you would like to be better at. What are they for you?

One thing is
CERTAIN:
IT'S HARD TO CHANGE
what we don't
ACKNOWLEDGE.

Each of us has a unique set of skills, abilities and experiences that we bring to any tough conversation. What's tough for one person may not be tough for another. Having the personal insight into which situations are particularly tough for you will help guide you towards making relevant changes in your behaviour. One thing is certain: we can't change what we don't acknowledge.

Finding out your tough stuff

To be able to prioritise what requires the greatest attention for improving results in your key conversations, rate yourself on the following questions and their corresponding continuums (see figure 1.1, overleaf).

Your answers to these seven questions will give you greater clarity on which tough-stuff situations you have strengths in, and which areas may need some attention. When you identify these areas to work on, you may be tempted to turn away from them because in the past you possibly avoided these situations. We urge you not to slip into old habits but to instead take the courage to change your approach.

Figure 1.1: rate your tough stuff

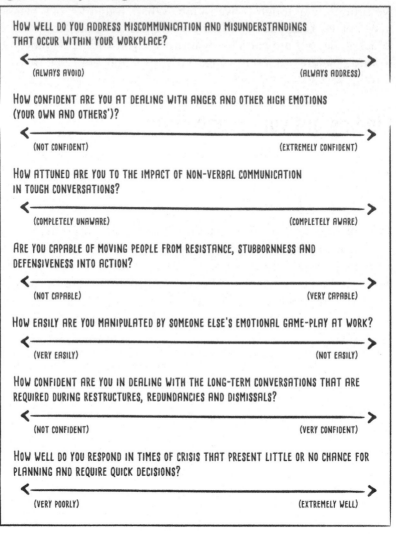

Vulnerability is the pathway to growth

As you move through the process of dealing with the tough stuff, at some point you will face a state of vulnerability. It's inevitable, and you should welcome it because it will set you on the road to success. Vulnerability is the readiness to take risks, to change behaviours and to do the 'right' thing, even in the face of uncertainty. Vulnerability is being okay with getting it wrong and making mistakes, particularly in front of your colleagues and co-workers. It's the courage to step up and try something that you believe is the right thing for your team, organisation and customers, even when you're unsure of what the outcome may be.

In a *Harvard Business Review* blog, Thomas J. DeLong, Professor of Management Practices at Harvard Business School, suggested that vulnerability plays a powerful role in behavioural change, both at an individual and at an organisational level. DeLong outlined a matrix that offers four options for performance. We have adapted DeLong's matrix to suit your individual process as you move through changing your behaviour and helping other people to change theirs (see figure 1.2, overleaf).

Figure 1.2: the vulnerability matrix

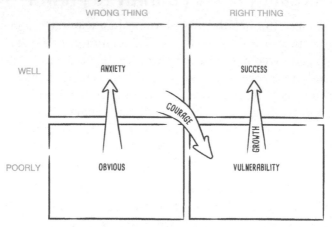

The vulnerability matrix is a simple quadrant model that provides four options for performance. In the column on the left, you have the opportunity to do the wrong thing well or the wrong thing poorly. And in the right-hand column, you have the choice to do the right thing well or poorly.

You will also notice that the bottom left quadrant is labelled 'Obvious'. Generally speaking, when we do something poorly and it isn't right for us it presents itself quite clearly as something that obviously needs to change.

The top left quadrant (doing something well that's not right for us) represents something that human beings can put up with for a very, very long time. Contrary to Sigmund Freud's main theories, people don't necessarily move away from anxiety: many can put up with it for years. Although we can be resilient in the face of anxiety, the cost can be considerable to our mental and physical states, as well as our relationships.

As with most quadrant models, most people aspire to be in the top right section, since doing the right thing well is assumed to lead to significant achievement. It makes sense that we would aim to master a skill and deliver it when needed. The challenge is making it to this quadrant. But as DeLong states, 'The only way to get there is through the bottom right quadrant. The only way you can do something well is to do something poorly first. There's no other way'.

We don't entirely agree with DeLong's absolute belief that the only way to reach the top right quadrant is through doing right things poorly (bottom right quadrant), as there are rare cases of naturals who don't have to achieve growth through failure. Some people just get it. But they're the minority, and the majority of us generally pay a toll for mastery through having to do the right thing poorly at least a few times.

Vulnerability is hard; doing things poorly is a risk. The easiest thing to do is continue doing the same thing you have always done and not allow yourself to be vulnerable. The problem with doing what you have always done is that you'll only achieve what you've always achieved. It's a much tougher option to actually change what you're doing: to try something new, such as a new direction, a new strategy, new technology, a new mindset or attitude, or even to have team meetings in a different location (sometimes the small changes can make a big difference). To change and know that, at first, things will feel weird and uncomfortable and that you'll feel a little vulnerable, is difficult. But it's the choice to move away from doing the wrong things well and towards doing the right things poorly that leads to the greatest reward.

Embracing vulnerability:
**WALKING AWAY
FROM THINGS**
you know well
IS THE SIMPLEST
DEFINITION
of COURAGE.

Unfortunately, most managers, supervisors and leaders in our organisations are reluctant to try something new for fear they will look silly, hesitant or even awkward. So a defensive mindset kicks in. They regress. And the result? They stick with what they know at the expense of taking risks, stretching themselves and being innovative. Our research shows that few people who focus on achievement, goals and outcomes (particularly short-term wins) would willingly entertain the idea of doing the right thing poorly. But to do so is to embrace vulnerability.

Your level of anxiety in embracing change is important to acknowledge, but you need to move your thinking towards embracing vulnerability rather than running away from it. Without being brave enough to take a risk, you won't get to this lower right quadrant. The reward is progressing to the upper right quadrant, to success and growth. That's where we play the game we really want to play — and play it well.

Moving away from doing the wrong thing well to doing the right thing poorly takes a huge amount of courage. In advance, congratulations for taking this significant step.

Conclusion

Being able to deal with the tough stuff starts with getting clear on what the tough stuff is for you personally. Knowing which conversations you may be avoiding at times but would like to be better at will bring a greater awareness to what you can change in these situations. Once you have some clarity about which key conversations you find tough, it's important to start being comfortable with being vulnerable. Taking the courageous step to changing your behaviours will be the pathway to growth and success.

Darren's insights

Apathy. That's my tough stuff. I don't mind anger, tears or other heightened emotions — I actually enjoy the energy that's present in those circumstances. But a noncommittal attitude, lack of ownership or inaction drives me crazy.

It would be easy for me just to avoid dealing with apathy. I can easily surround myself with people who have energy and passion. Yet, I have found that through dealing with my own tough stuff I have become good at dealing with apathy. In fact, colleagues say the way I deal with apathetic behaviour is a great strength. No-one is immune to the tough stuff, but we can all achieve successful outcomes by building our skills.

Alison's insights

For me the tough conversations are those that often do not have a clear right or wrong answer. Having a greater awareness about the conversations that I naturally avoid has helped me make a courageous choice to tackle them. The ancient Greek philosopher Socrates famously said 'know thyself', and in my personal and professional experience, I find the more individuals know themselves, the greater the chance for personal growth and change. It all starts here: get clear and specific on what's tough for you and make the courageous choice to tackle it.

Sean's insights

What riles me is when people say 'I can't'—a non-possibility mindset. I can handle 'I don't want to', but when people say 'I can't' it gets under my skin, probably because it seems to go against everything I stand for. I believe in people's potential, I believe there is more in a person than you can see in any given moment, and I believe we can always get better.

Similar to Darren, my life might be easier if I simply avoided the 'I can't-ers' and chose to align myself with only the positive, possibility thinkers, but I haven't. I have gone the other way and become a psychologist—a profession where I deal with the non-possibility mindset all the time.

I have survived by tackling my own tough stuff head-on, learning the skills of acceptance and empathy, and applying the tools in this book to help make a difference with those tough conversations I struggle with most. By confronting my tough stuff, I have found that I get to live within my purpose: there is nothing better for me than helping a person break through a limiting belief and transform from 'I can't' to 'I can'.

Chapter summary

- Identify the specific key conversations that you find tough. This will help you work out which areas need most attention.

- You will have to have key conversations—there's no way around it. Becoming skilled and confident at these conversations will see you succeed for years to come.

- Vulnerability means taking risks without knowing the outcome. It means being okay with making mistakes. Being equipped to deal with the tough stuff means being vulnerable at times.

- Moving away from doing the wrong thing well to doing the right thing poorly takes courage, and the rewards of this courageous step are success and growth.

- Remember that there are no perfect managers or leaders—we all make mistakes.

- Avoid procrastination, aim for perfection and be okay with 'perfectly good enough'.

HUMAN BEHAVIOUR

can be delightfully

MIND-BOGGLING.

2

DEALING WITH THE TOUGH STUFF
Foundational skills

As a leader, supervisor or manager, there's one inevitable task you will encounter: the tough-stuff conversation. Whether it's addressing underperformance, critiquing work or dealing with heightened emotions, some situations with some people will be tough — there's no escaping it.

Given that we can't avoid the tough conversations, a clear choice remains. The fact that these conversations are inevitable leaves us the options to:

- passively ignore them
- actively avoid them
- have them reluctantly
- get good at them.

We think the last option is by far your best choice if you plan to stay in a leadership or management role for longer than the next month or so, particularly if you want to be a leader with influence. If, on the other hand, you're a few weeks away from handing in your notice and heading to Tuscany to eat, drink and generally be merry, then perhaps you can get away with the first three options.

For the rest of us, who have to make do with reading about Tuscany (and occasionally sitting through a bad romantic comedy about a 50-something woman rediscovering her life) and turning up to work each day, there really isn't much choice. It's imperative to get good at the tough-stuff conversations because, quite simply, your leadership legacy is defined by how well you handle them.

The two steps to getting good at the tough conversations are:

- building a better understanding of human behaviour
- learning how to modify and influence the behaviour of others.

These are foundational skills that underlie the strategies and practices, but before they can be applied we need to unpack some basic principles about why we do what we do.

Why do we do what we do?

Human behaviour can be mind-boggling at times. For every example of strength, bravery, courage and heroism in the world there are as many acts of stupidity, irrationality and downright bizarreness. Yet all behaviour can be understood in the context within which it's exhibited. At some point in our lives we have all been flabbergasted by someone's behaviour and asked ourselves, 'Why do people act this way?' or thought, 'I don't understand why they have done this'. But it's worth considering the broader context to understand the why behind the what.

ABC model of human behaviour

Understanding why people behave the way they do can be tricky and has essentially spawned the science of psychology. Despite human behaviour being incredibly complex and diverse, the building

14

blocks of behaviour (what we do) are best understood through a simple yet effective tool known as the ABC model.

The ABC model breaks down and segments behaviour in order to understand it better in the same way that an editor pulls sentences apart and considers each word on its own. If you've ever studied psychology or read books on behaviour modification, you will have encountered this model. It's back-to-basics psychology, but it provides a great platform for investigating what else is at play when we're exploring human behaviour. When dealing with the tough stuff, understanding the context of someone's behaviour is important and will lead to greater success in your ability to influence that behaviour.

The ABC model of human behaviour (see figure 2.1) considers behaviour across three elements:

- *Antecedents*. Events that occur or are present before the person performs the behaviour.

- *Behaviour*. What the person did, or what can be directly observed in the present.

- *Consequences*. Events that occur after and as a result of the behaviour.

Figure 2.1: the ABC model of behaviour

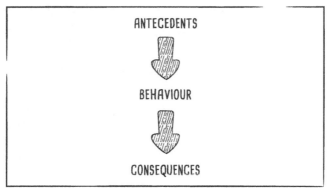

'Antecedents' is just a fancy word for 'what comes before'. It describes the environment, conditions or factors that occur before a behaviour. Then the behaviour itself occurs and the consequences stem from that. For example, feeling tired is an *antecedent* for sleeping, sleeping is the *behaviour* and feeling rested the next day is a *consequence* of sleeping.

Taking this a step further, feeling rested may then become the *antecedent* for delivering a clear and powerful pitch to a new client (*behaviour*), which results in securing new business (*consequence*). This is how a consequence of a behaviour can become an antecedent of future behaviour: one flows from the next to the next, and so on, becoming a continuing pattern.

Understanding this pattern is integral for managers because the consequences you apply in the workplace become powerful predictors of whether or not someone will continue with a particular behaviour.

Essentially, the ABC model says that to affect behaviour (your own or that of others) you can change any of these three factors and the outcome will be directly affected.

Table 2.1 shows how managers can affect behaviour to achieve different outcomes.

Table 2.1: examples of how a manager can affect the elements of antecedents, behaviour and consequences

	What happened	How this could be changed
Antecedent	Argument between two team members in the morning	Intervene during the disagreement and seek a resolution then and there
Behaviour	They don't speak to each other at the team meeting	Use strategic questioning to ensure both parties contribute at the meeting, removing the impasse
Consequence	The project they're working on together is stalled because they won't work together, and other staff complain	Address the two team members and seek a resolution to the disagreement. Gather the rest of the team and ensure their commitment to moving the project forward

By understanding that there are antecedents (things that come before a behaviour) and consequences (things that come after a behaviour) you come to understand why people do certain things and, more usefully, why they keep doing them again and again. The antecedents and consequences provide the all-important context for understanding behaviours.

Let's look at an example of someone being drunk at a party. What are some possible antecedents to this behaviour? What are the things that led to someone being drunk at a party?

Reasons may include that they did not eat before the party, or that they drink to deal with their shyness, or that they drink when they feel angry or upset. The reasons may be social antecedents, such as peer pressure, or the drunkenness may simply be the result of consuming a lot of alcohol. It could also be all of these things occurring simultaneously. Our subject, who has had one too many, could be a shy person who's being peer pressured, hasn't had anything to eat and has drunk too much, all at the same time.

Importantly, there are *always* multiple antecedents for any behaviour.

Now, what might be some of the consequences of this behaviour?

The consequences might be a headache or injury, the person might embarrass themselves, or they might have a great time at the party—or the consequences might be all of the above. It could be like the movie *The Hangover*, in which there are plenty of consequences linked to this behaviour: a hangover that measures 9.5 on the Richter scale, no recollection of the night whatsoever, a very unfortunate tattoo and Mike Tyson's tiger in the bathroom!

As with antecedents, there are *always* multiple consequences for any behaviour.

Exploring antecedents

As a workplace manager or leader, at some point you will need to make changes to other people's behaviours: increased workload, fewer mistakes, greater ownership of a project, or even something as simple as asking a staff member to smile more at the front counter.

The behavioural coaching you do as a manager is a vitally important component of your work.

Your success in shifting or modifying a person's behaviour is directly related to how well you understand the antecedent structure that drives the behaviour itself. You could brainstorm several strategies on how to get someone to smile at the front counter, yet if we don't know the reasons (the antecedents) for a person not smiling, they may not stand a chance of succeeding.

Given there are always multiple antecedents for any behaviour, let's look at a case study to see how understanding antecedents may help create a better resolution of a problem.

Case study: Tali and Rex

Tali is Rex's supervisor. While Rex is generally productive and a great contributor to the team, lately his standards have been slipping. Over the past month he has started coming to work late and he sometimes leaves early; he shows little initiative in his work and seldom puts his hand up for projects. This is out of character for Rex. Tali invites him into her office and, in a very professional manner, addresses two key areas she'd like him to improve on because his current work, she says, is 'not up to scratch'. Those areas are: number one, punctuality; and number two, accountability for his project-work time frames.

Rex quietly listens to what Tali has to say and admits he hasn't been as motivated as usual. He agrees with the points Tali has raised, says he will try to do his best to improve things and walks out. Tali isn't convinced by Rex's body language (including the way he looked at the floor and the way he turned away from her and angled his body towards the door). Her fears are confirmed when Rex doesn't turn up to work the next day, having phoned in sick.

In an informal conversation with Debbie, Rex's closest friend at work, Tali discovers Rex has been suffering from depression and has been struggling with his medication and his mood.

Notice what is out of character

People don't change their behaviour unless something prompts the change. Here is one of the biggest of many big takeaway lessons from this book:

> *If there's been a change in a person's behaviour, there must have been a change in the antecedent structure.*

Written in plain–speak: if you've noticed a change in someone's behaviour, then something must be driving the change.

And here's the kicker: the clearer you can be about the drivers for change, the clearer you will be in shaping behavioural change and influencing a more desirable behaviour.

In the case study, Tali addressed Rex's behaviour directly, an admirable course of action. But she could have mapped out a better strategy, or at the very least managed the situation better by exploring the antecedents that may have driven the recent change in Rex's behaviour. By starting the conversation along the lines of, 'Rex, I've noticed a change in your usual high standards. Is there any reason behind why you're not as punctual as usual, or why you haven't been putting your hand up for project work?' Tali could have opened the door for Rex to share the antecedents that may be contributing towards his changed behaviour.

You will not always get answers, but in many cases you will. By simply addressing the behaviours without first considering the antecedents that drive the behaviour (as Tali initially did), we lock ourselves into a behaviour–change strategy that may not match the antecedents that are present.

By considering what else is going on in a person's life, you can begin to understand the broader context of their behaviour. Wherever possible, look at other factors that may be antecedents, because this understanding will help deliver a better outcome.

Behaviour modification

One of the roles of any manager is to influence, guide, support, adjust and ultimately modify the behaviour of others. In a nutshell, behaviour modification is the use of specific techniques aimed at increasing or decreasing certain behaviours.

What is critically important for effective management is to recognise and be conscious of the strategies you're currently employing. You are influencing and modifying the behaviour of others, but you may not be conscious of the strategies you're using. That makes it difficult to know how to repeat a strategy if it works, or what to change if it doesn't. What's important is to learn how to be strategic about influencing the behaviour of those you are managing in the most effective manner.

The two strategies used widely in modifying human behaviour are:

- reinforcement
- punishment.

While many people recognise these two terms, few understand the correct time and context for employing them effectively.

What do we mean by reinforcement and punishment?

Most people associate the terms 'reinforcement' and 'punishment' with good and bad, positive and negative. These are the social definitions often connected to these words, but they're not true definitions.

This misunderstanding is a bit like our misunderstanding of the words 'extrovert' and 'introvert'. Most people think the extrovert is the really loud person, the life of the party who always has a crowd around them and is over the top; and the introvert is the quiet, shy bookworm who likes to sit in a corner and do their own thing, and generally likes being left alone. That's how extroverts and introverts are defined socially, but the true definitions of those two words—particularly when Carl Jung, the founder of analytical psychology, popularised them—actually relate to where our energy comes from. Extroverts get their energy from the world around them: people, hobbies, things, other interests, and so on. Introverts, on the other hand, gain their energy from their inner world of thoughts and ideas. The true definition is decidedly different from the social definition.

Back to reinforcement and punishment. They aren't good and bad, and they aren't positive and negative. All these terms mean is simply to increase the occurrence of a behaviour (reinforcement), or decrease or eliminate the occurrence of a behaviour (punishment). They're not good and bad, there's no judgement around them: they mean simply to do 'more of' or 'less of'.

Two types of reinforcement

Reinforcement comes in two forms: positive and negative. The positive and negative do not mean good and bad, but addition and subtraction: to add or remove something to the circumstance to see an increase in the occurrence of a behaviour.

Positive reinforcement

So let's start with a very common term, positive reinforcement, and look at each component.

- 'Positive' means to add something to the situation.
- 'Reinforcement' aims to increase the desired behaviour.

In simple terms, a positive reinforcement strategy is one that adds something else to the equation in order to see more of the desired behaviour.

So what's the most common and arguably the best positive reinforcer known to mammals? Yep—you got it: praise (congratulations!).

Praise works phenomenally well on human beings and other mammals. If you have a dog, you know where we're coming from. Your pooch will almost starve itself for praise. And human beings will do the same. In a desert of praise we will drink the sand—it's such a key driver for us.

Other common positive reinforcers are food, rewards, money, gifts, responsibility, attention—almost anything you can add to a situation to see more of the desired behaviour.

Research about the use of different forms of praise has been done over the past 20 years, championed by Stanford researcher Carol Dweck. She reminds us that not only is praise a good thing, but certain types of praise are also far more effective in creating success in the long term. Dweck and her colleagues pointed to a phenomenon they called the 'effort effect'—heaps of praise for the right behaviours and the quality of effort that goes into those behaviours, rather than praise for innate ability, intelligence or talent.

With regard to persistence, it turns out that when people are praised for effort, and believe that effort is the key determinant of success, they see failure as an opportunity for learning. When people are praised for their natural abilities, and believe that talent is the key determinant of success, they see failure as a reason to give up. The key is to praise people not only for the outcome but for the effort they have put into a task, and they will persist at it through barriers.

In short, giving positive reinforcement for behaviours within a person's control, rather than praising natural ability that is predetermined and out of their control, is far more effective. In professional sport you learn very quickly that if you don't regularly reinforce the behaviours you want to see on the ground, you may as well congratulate the other team on their win before the game has even started. To ensure your team wins the game, you need to reinforce regularly.

Negative reinforcement

Negative reinforcement is less common, but it is still effective and occurs in our workplaces regularly. Again, breaking down the two words that make up the term helps us gain clarity.

- 'Negative' means to remove something from the situation.
- 'Reinforcement' aims to increase the desired behaviour.

So, negative reinforcement is removing something to see more of the desired behaviour. Negative reinforcers are a lot rarer than positive ones, but they are still enormously effective.

You will see negative reinforcement at work if you have graduates, trainees or apprentices in your organisation. When they finish their traineeship or their apprenticeship it seems that, the moment you take away their probationary status, they step out as almost a new person — ready and confident to use their new tools.

In this case, it's the removal of something (probation) to see more of a desired behaviour (ownership or responsibility). Some organisations remove set working hours and introduce flexible hours because some people (such as those with family responsibilities) work better at certain times of the day. This is another way of getting more of something by taking something away. Removing the set working hours increases productivity and morale.

REINFORCEMENT:

making it

RANDOM

keeps it

RELEVANT!

Two types of punishment

The aim of punishment, on the other hand, is to see less of a behaviour or to eliminate it. Again, we have both positive and negative punishments, and once again positive and negative mean to add or remove something respectively.

Positive punishment

Positive punishment sounds weird, doesn't it? That's because it doesn't match the social definition — it seems to be saying bad and good don't go together. Again, if we look at the two words independently the definition becomes clearer.

- 'Positive' means to add something to the situation.
- 'Punishment' aims to decrease or eliminate the undesired behaviour.

So while positive punishment sounds weird, we can see it's actually an everyday part of our work as a leader. In fact, you probably use it every single day!

The classic form of positive punishment is critique: 'Not a bad job but if we could take out those spelling mistakes and those typos, Gabriel, that would be great'.

So it's adding something (commentary) to see 'less of' something (mistakes). As managers and supervisors we actually use positive punishment quite a lot. It shouldn't be a moral judgement that someone has done something wrong, as may be implied by the word 'punishment'.

Negative punishment

The final area to consider in these basic behaviour modification strategies is negative punishment.

- 'Negative' means to remove something from the situation.
- 'Punishment' aims to decrease or eliminate the undesired behaviour.

Negative punishment in the workplace is usually pretty severe. It's when we take something away to see 'less of' something. It may be taking away responsibility or wages or it may actually be sacking someone. This is the ultimate form of negative punishment in the workplace: we don't want a certain behaviour to happen any more so we take the person away. That's the ultimate way of making sure that behaviour doesn't happen anymore.

Getting clear

Most people inadvertently use these strategies, although they're usually not sure when and where they're using them. Some executives we coach have made comments such as, 'I'm confused. I sat down with Joanne and told her I need her to be on time to team meetings and that her lateness isn't going to be tolerated any longer. That if she continues to turn up late there'll be consequences'. At this point a smile starts creeping across our lips because we know what's coming next.

'Then she turned up to the next team meeting and just sat there, pouting. Just sat there, didn't do anything. Unbelievable!'

Our reply? 'You got what you asked for.'

What you've asked her for is 'less of' (lateness) and so you're also going to get 'less of' in a whole bunch of other areas (contribution in the meeting, for example) until the time comes when you can reinforce the behaviours and get her doing 'more of' again.

Collateral effect

One of our favourite sayings is, 'A rising tide lifts all ships'. And this is what happens with reinforcement and punishment. If we use a reinforcer, we actually see other behaviours increase across the board. So if you do a good job and I'm your boss and I say, 'Oh, awesome job!', positively reinforcing the behaviours, I will actually see a rise in other behaviours elsewhere.

If I said to someone else, 'That's not good enough, and it's really not what we do around here, so next time can you make sure there are no mistakes like this?', there's a strong likelihood we will see a drop in behaviours in all aspects of an employee's work.

Be mindful of the strategy you're using, because there are increases and decreases, not just on that singular behaviour, but in other areas as well. In the case of the executive's conversation with Joanne, getting Joanne to do 'more of' rather than 'less of' may be a better conversation to have. Instead of rebuking her for being late (positive punishment), the boss could assign the first agenda item in the next meeting to Joanne (so she has to be there on time) and reinforce the behaviour through praise (positive reinforcement) when she achieves the task.

Lead strategy

We believe that a high-performing workplace should have a ratio of 90 per cent reinforcement to 10 per cent punishment. Where do you think your current ratio sits? What about the ratio across your workplace?

You may have assessed this at different levels: some teams may be 80/20, some more like 50/50 and some may be more like 20/80. And all of those ratios may be serving the purpose intended. The reason we suggest the 90/10 rule—and remember we prefixed the statement with the words 'high-performing workplace'—is because these workplaces ask people to work harder, faster, smarter. And these are all 'more of' behaviours—more efficient, more innovative, more productive. In the high-performing workplace, our lead strategy should be reinforcement, not punishment.

These ratios are flipped in some workplaces, albeit at a cost. For instance, if a new manager walks into a 'zero harm' workplace, which requires zero tolerance for unsafe practices, and people are operating in an unsafe or dangerous manner, they need to eliminate that behaviour. But in taking on punishment as a lead strategy, productivity is going to drop, along with other behaviours across the board. This is why many workplaces are now using behavioural safety interventions to drive safer work practices. These are programs that focus upon the thought processes involved when someone chooses to undertake a safe or unsafe act—in short, a safer workplace without the impact of the lost productivity or lost output that would accompany the implementation of punishment as a lead strategy.

Similarly, if you use reinforcement as your dominant strategy, there's going to be an increase in behaviours across the board and sometimes that actually may include things such as skylarking, or taking more risks, or similar behaviours. How many times have you seen someone rising up the corporate ladder and really going places—so they're getting reinforced a lot—and suddenly they step outside the boundary. For example, they create a policy on the run and send an email out to the entire network without first getting it signed off by their manager. Be mindful of your lead strategy, but be prepared to work with some collateral behaviours that will occur as a result.

Ensure maximum effectiveness

It's not enough to know how reinforcement and punishment work as behaviour modification strategies in our workplace. We also need to ensure maximum effectiveness of the strategies we use. What's really interesting about the words 'maximum' and 'effectiveness' is that there's a best-practice code that goes with them. The schedule for how reinforcement should be applied is shown in figure 2.2.

Figure 2.2: the reinforcement schedule

If there doesn't appear to be a pattern, then you are correct! Reinforcement works best when it's intermittent and can't be predicted. Once a reinforcement schedule can be predicted it starts to lose its motivational effect.

Take poker machines, for example. Why are they so effective? Why do people feed their wages into them at clubs and pubs? It's because of the pokies' intermittent schedule, or reinforcement pattern. They work so well because players don't know when the machine is going to pay out, and they don't know how big the payout will be. Most problem gamblers have a couple of wins early on, which deludes them into thinking they can work the game out. They will also sit back and watch someone else using up all the bad spins and pounce on the machine like a jaguar the minute the person moves off it.

From poker machines to the workplace: if you want to get reinforcement schedules working really well, they should be implemented without rhyme or reason. Contrary to popular belief, Christmas bonuses actually aren't strong reinforcers. They are in the first year, but after that they just slip into a pattern of expectation. The same is also true for performance reviews that are attached to monetary bonuses—they're not effective motivators because the process is too predictable. This is one reason why we're seeing a shift away from purely monetary incentives—because they become an expectation rather than a reinforcer.

Praise is our best friend in managing and leading other people when it is used intermittently. For example, at the end of a project that Allan has put six months of his life into, don't say, 'Yeah, good job, Allan,' and walk off. He is thinking, 'Is that it?' Whereas Jo, who's been working on a spreadsheet for six minutes, doesn't expect to hear, 'Everyone! Look at what Jo's done! It's fabulous!' Ensure your praise matches the circumstances and you'll achieve intermediate patterning. Allan's praise should be big praise! It could be anything ranging from a nomination for a public award through to a handwritten letter of gratitude for his work. Remember, small things can have a very big impact. Every situation is different, so the guiding principle is to dial up the praise for the big stuff and dial it down for the little stuff.

Consistently inconsistent

You need to be random in your use of reinforcers to achieve the best effect because consistency can reduce the effectiveness of a reinforcer.

Let's say you are appointed the new CEO of a medium-sized organisation where the previous boss was a tyrant. She was one of those bosses where you would hear her footsteps in the hallway and everyone would cringe—a *Devil Wears Prada* kind of boss.

As the new boss you tell yourself you're not going to be like the previous scary CEO. That's your first order of business. At the end of the first Monday you walk out into the open-plan office and say, 'Thanks very much guys! It's been an awesome day working with you, and we're really doing some awesome stuff here. See you again tomorrow'. And off you go.

Everyone thinks, 'Oh, that was nice, not like the old DWP (*Devil Wears Prada*) boss'.

At the end of Tuesday you come out and say, 'Right guys, we're off home, thanks again. Gee we've done some fantastic work. We really got off to a great start in the week. See you all tomorrow'.

Do you see what happens to that reinforcer by Friday? It just becomes a greeting and loses its impact because it's too consistent. So make sure that you reinforce inconsistently and you punish consistently.

Consistently consistent

As you can see in figure 2.3, the pattern for punishment is again a schedule, and it's not really complicated.

Figure 2.3: the punishment schedule

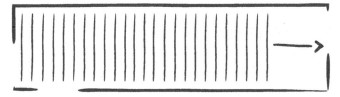

For punishment to work as a strategy it has to have a consistent pattern of use. The basic rule of thumb for punishment as an effective strategy is that it has to be applied:

- immediately
- every time
- for as long as it takes.

The moment this consistent pattern turns into an inconsistent pattern, it mirrors the best reinforcement pattern and loses effectiveness. We actually reinforce the behaviour that we're trying to avoid.

Some of you may have inherited failed punishment strategies, where someone has started a punishment style and then given up, or stopped and then started again. Repeat half a dozen times and you have yourself a very resistant-to-change behaviour because it's been reinforced over a length of time.

So, punishment is a tough gig. Any parent will know just how hard it can be to stay consistent in addressing behaviours you don't want to see. It's exhausting!

It's the same in the workplace: if you're going to use punishment, commit to the schedule of consistency and see it out. It's tough, but if you don't see it through to the end, you simply get 'more of' the very thing you want to see less of. Particularly in public-sector and large organisations, and policy-heavy workplaces, it can sometimes take years to undo the damage caused by an inconsistent punishment schedule.

Although we suggest punishment works extremely well when used the right way, we also realise that punishment as a strategy is tough work and can drain both energy and resources. So we suggest another strategy, where you can avoid punishment altogether: competing behaviours.

Competing behaviours

A competing behaviour is where we take a desired behaviour that's incompatible with an undesirable behaviour and overlay it in the circumstance.

Let's say you're a cigarette smoker and you decide that this year is the year you're going to give up. So you go to the doctor and say, 'I really want to kick this habit. What's the best way to move forward?' One of the first things the doctor will advise? Do more exercise.

Why? Because it's a classic competing behaviour. You can't really go out for a jog and smoke at the same time. If you did, a smart doctor would suggest taking up swimming! You'd have to be really inventive to smoke and swim at the same time, wouldn't you?

A workplace example of the competing behaviour strategy may be someone whose work consistently has grammar and spelling mistakes throughout it. Sure, you could go down the punishment pathway to reduce the number of mistakes, or you could look for a competing behaviour that could be used.

A desired behaviour would be for the person to employ a double-check system where they, first, print the document off for reading (diligence); and, second, give it to a peer for proofreading (collaboration) before submitting it.

Rather than using a punishment, we replace the unwanted behaviour with desired behaviours that compete directly against it. In this case, if the staff member uses diligence and collaboration (the desired behaviours) they make fewer, if any, mistakes (undesired behaviour).

Instead of punishing the behaviour, look for something you want from the person (desired behaviour) that competes with the undesired behaviour.

Meaningful work

Reinforcement, punishment and the use of a competing behaviour are three broad areas to focus on when effecting behavioural change. They all work well given the right context, but all are disabled as effective processes in the modern workplace when people lose a sense of meaning in their work. Sure, if it's a factory setting, these principles will still hold weight, but if you need higher order concepts, such as lateral thinking, problem solving and innovation from your staff, then ensuring people have an attachment to the general purpose of their work is critical.

Employees who are engaged in meaningful work get things done. It's as simple as that. International best-selling author and staff writer for the *New Yorker* magazine Malcolm Gladwell says three things are needed to create meaningful work (see figure 2.4).

- *Complexity.* The work needs to have a level of complexity to be challenging.

- *Autonomy.* Individuals need the space to be able to do what needs to be done their way.

- *Relationship between effort and reward.* Is it clear and transparent that if you put in effort there will be an equivalent reward?

By the way, an expected and predicted yearly bonus that's based on whether the business has enough money rather than the effort put in doesn't create meaningful work. This type of bonus quickly becomes an expectation rather than a reward.

Figure 2.4: the three things needed to create meaningful work

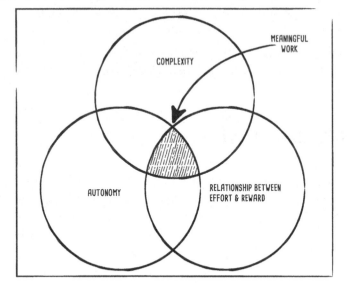

Conclusion

Great leaders are those who continue to develop and grow. The ability to address and confront the tough stuff is directly related to your ability to learn, grow and develop. Understanding the foundations of why people do what they do, and knowing where to start when the need to deal with the tough stuff arises, is fundamental.

Remember to focus on the end goals and match your behaviour-modification strategies to them. Once you are clear on the direction, the steps required become much easier.

Darren's insights

Understanding human behaviours should be a core competency for managers rather than an afterthought. The difference-makers in any organisation are the frontline managers, yet the biggest difference they can make—through understanding how people behave—is often an area of least attention.

It's baffling how little time is spent in organisations building human skills in the management and leadership layer. Recent labour force statistics from the United States show that more than 80 per cent of the labour market is now in the service industry, yet organisations consistently promote and reward technical skills over human skills. We still build our leaders on a manufacturing-based approach, and yet we require our staff to be people-centric customer service champions. There's a huge disconnect that needs to be remedied.

Alison's insights

Why people do what they do is a complex and complicated web. But managing with your head in the sand and living for years on end with the consequences of unresolved tension or conflict can be even tougher, and certainly far more costly, than taking on the tough stuff. The price you pay in the workplace is loss of productivity, loss of morale, dissatisfaction and disengagement, to name a few.

The price you pay with your own health, however, can be huge. Stress-related disorders, depression, anxiety and poor sleep are all symptoms I see in clients who have come to me because of unresolved workplace issues. How do we resolve these issues in therapy? By exploring human behaviours through the lenses we have covered in this chapter. If you have unresolved workplace conflict or tension, review this chapter again with that filter in place. It may make you a whole lot healthier.

Sean's insights

The principles of looking deeper into the drivers of human behaviour, captured in the ABC model, are simple but ridiculously important—although they are often disregarded in the context of tough-stuff conversations. Too many people seem to want an outcome without putting the time or effort into understanding.

Step back, take your time and navigate the complexity of a tough conversation. Examine the antecedents and apply the most effective reinforcement or punishment strategy for the situation, rather than taking the easy way out and avoiding the conversation altogether, or blasting straight through it.

Going deeper into understanding human beings and changing your own behaviour will create resistance at times—the survival part of our brains is designed to take the shortest path between two objects, even if the longer path may give a better outcome. It's an efficiency principle about playing it safe, and it is designed to keep you alive in a threatening world, so you will have to battle your survival instincts if you want to do this stuff right.

Chapter summary

- The ABC model of human behaviour explains why people do things through understanding antecedents (what comes before), behaviour (what's happening now) and consequences (what comes after).

- The two key forms of behaviour modification are punishment and reinforcement. Punishment is used to get others to do less of something, and reinforcement is used to get others to do more of something.

- There are two types of punishment and two types of reinforcement: positive and negative. 'Positive' in this context means to 'add', and 'negative' means to 'take away'.

- Praise is a powerful and effective positive reinforcement strategy.

- Make sure your strategy matches the goal. If you want greater productivity (more of certain behaviours), use reinforcement. If you want to reduce mistakes (less of certain behaviours), then perhaps punishment is a good option.

- The use of competing behaviours (replacing an undesired behaviour with a desired behaviour) can be used if you want to avoid using punishment.

- Good leaders use a mix of behaviour modification techniques—reinforcement, punishment and competing behaviours—ensuring they have a lead strategy.

Great leaders

CHALLENGE

THE BEHAVIOUR, BUT

SUPPORT

THE PERSON.

3

DEALING WITH
THE FLUFF STUFF

Getting more direct
in your language and
achieving clarity

Remember how cool it was, as a kid, to get your hands on some bubble wrap? Popping those little pockets of air was great fun, wasn't it? Sometimes you'd pop all the bubbles in the first five minutes, but other times you'd make the fun last for ages. Once the bubbles were all popped, however, you were just left with plastic—damaged plastic that no longer served any purpose.

Sometimes we wonder if our society is still just as fascinated with bubble wrap, even though we've moved on from our childhood fascinations. We love to wrap things up in a protective covering rather than deal with the bumps and bruises that give our lives character. We avoid the trials and tribulations—the same things we pay good money to see in movies on the big screen.

Conflict and disagreement are unavoidable and they should often be celebrated rather than condemned. History shows some of the greatest inventions, civil movements and advances in humanity have occurred as a direct result of two or more people butting heads.

Despite this, we love to wrap reality in cotton wool. We do it through our actions, our behaviours and, mostly, through our words. Interestingly, it is our complex language that provides far too many options for fluff. The very nature of the English language can lend itself to misunderstanding and conjecture.

Too often the tough situations are avoided or amplified because communication is unclear. What is said can be easily misinterpreted and misconstrued because of the words and language used. The age-old cliché, 'It's not what you say, it's how you say it', is not quite right. A more correct version may be, 'It is what you say and how you say it'.

The way you say things (your non-verbal communication) is discussed in chapter 4, with a specific section dedicated to the art of using your eyes, voice and body to achieve better results.

In this chapter we'll explore the verbal communication skills required to get direct in your language and achieve greater clarity of expectations. If you've ever had a conversation with someone where you thought they understood what you said but they walked away and did the complete opposite, then you'll want to read on.

Get rid of the fluff

When we have to deal with the tough stuff, we often fluff around the subject and avoid being clear and getting to the point. Others around us also use fluff. How many acronyms are used in your organisation? Do you have a secret jargon? In this era of FYI, BCC, LOL and OMG we sometimes sit comfortably behind fluff and avoid getting down to the key issue.

To get rid of the fluff you have to get clear in your communication, get clear in your intent and get to the point.

When we're having robust conversations at work, the language we use can personalise a situation very quickly. While the process of personalising a conversation is critically important when building rapport and maintaining relationships, in the tough-stuff conversations personalisation is a fast-track to heightened conflict. The best way of depersonalising a conversation or a point that you need to make with someone is to speak in terms of specific behaviours rather than in terms of broad traits.

Traits versus behaviours

Your ability to remove the fluff, confusion and assumptions that arise in conversations comes from stepping out of using traits and gaining clarity through desired behaviours.

Do you know people who you'd describe as adventurous, lazy or unreliable? These descriptors are traits. A trait is merely a label, usually a descriptor of a combination of behaviours. For example, if someone is considered courteous, that would be a trait. It's a convenient way to describe a collection of behaviours, such as holding a door open for someone, wishing people good morning or asking people if they would like anything at the shops. A behaviour is something that's directly observable. A trait is usually a combination of behaviours.

Why focus on behaviours in the tough stuff?

Traits are important in our language. Could you imagine if we didn't have a way to describe collective behaviours? We would spend all day describing specific details and behaviours.

But there are two main reasons why it's important to identify behaviour rather than refer to traits when dealing with the tough stuff. The first is that confusion occurs easily when we talk in traits. The reason for this confusion is that the definition of what constitutes a certain trait varies from person to person. Let's explain further.

Say you introduce someone you know really well to a group of your friends. 'Hey guys, this is Simon. He's a great guy, and is one of the most generous people I know.'

In that introduction we've named two traits: 'great guy' and 'generous'. Let's focus on generous. If you give it some thought, there are hundreds of behaviours we could expect to see from someone who is generous. One of your friends might define generosity as giving money to charities. Another friend might define a generous person as someone who volunteers their time at a local library, while another might see them as a person who mentors others via their experience. These are just three of a multitude of possible variations on behaviours within generosity.

There is a danger, particularly in a tough-stuff conversation, that you can be naming a trait and the other person is sitting there nodding in agreement, but their agreement is based on a different definition from yours. Making sure you speak in terms of behavioural language when having a tough-stuff conversation is incredibly important—it means that you're both operating on a shared understanding.

Case study: Bernice

Bernice and her manager were having her performance review discussion. As part of this meeting Bernice's manager provided some feedback: 'You know, by and large, Bernice, you're doing a good job. I think over the next couple of months what you could work on is being more methodical'.

Bernice defined being methodical in these terms:

- Creating more to-do lists.
- Keeping a diary (which she wasn't doing).
- Being more organised.

Following this meeting she bought a new diary and started writing a to-do list every morning. She made a real effort to be more methodical, according to her definition. She felt she was on her way to meeting her manager's request.

About a month after the conversation, Bernice received a fairly short phone call from her manager saying, 'Bernice I need to see you in my office immediately'.

Bernice went into the office and her manager said, 'What's this?' In the manager's hand was a press briefing Bernice had written earlier that morning. 'It's not in the style set in our style guide, which changed three weeks ago,' said the very annoyed manager.

Bernice immediately recognised her mistake, apologised profusely and assured her boss the press briefing would be put into the correct style and would be back on the manager's desk in 15 minutes.

Her manager then said, 'I thought we talked only about a month ago about you being more methodical in your work'.

Here we see the grey area. The manager's definition of 'methodical' was adherence to established processes — nothing to do with Bernice's understanding of being more organised.

Bernice started to realise there was a difference in interpretations and expectations. The two were then able to have a discussion about specific behaviours that the manager was seeking from Bernice. Armed with this new clarity of expectation, Bernice was able to meet her manager's expectations.

The second reason why it's important to identify behaviours rather than traits is that studies have shown that traits are more difficult to change than behaviours. Traits are usually enduring patterns of behaviour that can be formed as far back as childhood, so thinking you can effectively change a trait in a 30-minute feedback session is more than a little ambitious. In dealing with the tough stuff, start with behaviours rather than traits and you'll have a higher chance of success.

A key goal when dealing with tough situations is often a change in behaviour. You want people to do something differently: more of something, less of something or something totally new. Ensuring that you describe specific behaviours in your language makes it far easier for someone to know what you want changed, including when and how that behaviour is to be demonstrated.

Sometimes we naturally put both traits and behaviours into our language. If you listen to people you will notice they automatically say things like, 'I need you to take control of this project. If you could email everyone with dates for completing actions, that would be great'. The trait of 'take control' has been followed by a specific example of the behaviour you're after (email everyone with dates). This makes your expectation very clear.

The dilemma is that we often forget to do this when we're under the pressure of a tough-stuff conversation. The reality, however, is that this is the very moment that we need to be more specific in our conversations, and not less. And clarity in conversations comes from talking about behaviours rather than traits.

Table 3.1 lists four trait phrases and breaks these down into a handful of behaviours we might expect to see from somebody.

Table 3.1: four traits and possible associated behaviours

Traits	Behaviours
Sound work ethic	• stayed back late to complete a project in July
	• completes tasks to agreed time frames
	• looks for extra work when own workload has eased off
	• completes work to a high standard
Good team worker	• assisted with Jack's induction last month
	• was available to cover reception duties when required, without needing to be asked
	• uses positive language when communicating with other team members
	• contributes at team meetings, putting ideas forward
Needs to be more methodical	• lack of lists and calendars for planning workload
	• occasional mistakes in end-of-month reporting
	• new tasks distract Jules from completion of old ones

Traits	Behaviours
Could take more initiative	• rarely puts hand up to lead projects
	• has not come forward with any future learning and development requests
	• neglected to finish assigned tasks when manager was away for two weeks' leave

Table 3.1 is an excellent planning tool for the tough-stuff conversations. Think broadly in terms of traits, write them down and then break those traits into the specific behaviours you're looking for. Use this table to get clear on your points before having a tough conversation — it's particularly useful for performance review discussions.

Remember that change can be more easily effected in behaviours than traits.

Given the opportunity, most people do the right thing

Removing the fluff and confusion from our intent and being able to say what is often merely assumed forms one of the skills key to being effective in dealing with the tough stuff. The reality is that most people, when given a choice between a positive outcome and a negative outcome, will steer their behaviour towards the positive outcome. Most people like to be liked and will act in a way that will encourage being liked. In the vast majority of cases, people will drive their own behaviour modification in pursuit of the positive outcome if they are given a choice.

We know that some people in the workplace do choose the negative outcome, using wilful and considered disobedience or defiance. So why do they choose this behaviour?

The only reason people will choose a known negative outcome over a positive outcome is that they believe the payoff in the negative outcome *must* be greater than the payoff in the positive outcome.

The payoff for negative behaviour can manifest itself in workplaces where the primary currency for people in the workplace is attention; they seek attention above all else. They may wilfully choose the negative outcome because the attention they receive as a result is actually greater than the attention they get for doing the right thing. It's like the well-known saying, 'The squeaky wheel gets the oil'. (This is explored further in chapter 7.) In essence, if you move the attention away from the undesirable behaviour and start reinforcing the desirable behaviours of these individuals, you'll start to see a shift in this tendency. If we make our language, and as a result our expectations, clearer, people will often choose the behaviour required to achieve the outcome you want, rather than you having to dictate it to them.

Case study: specifying behaviours

Tim is considered to be lazy (trait) by his co-workers. Despite being told he is a lazy employee, and his manager regularly asking him to pull his finger out, there have been few changes to Tim's day-to-day work output over a six-month period.

In order to help improve Tim's work output, his manager needs to concentrate on the behaviours that combine to label him with the trait of laziness. Tim's manager comes up with this list:

- tardiness in starting work

- not finishing projects in accordance with agreed deadlines

- allowing other team members to perform his tasks for him

- not contributing in team meetings.

By addressing these specific behaviours with Tim, rather than talking about laziness, Tim is more likely to modify his trait of laziness through his behaviours. Describing behaviours in a tough-stuff conversation also depersonalises the situation, reducing the likelihood of Tim getting defensive, shutting down and taking it personally.

Stepping into behaviour-based language

Unpacking, recognising and adapting the language that you use at work can feel a bit weird to start with. You may feel like you're simply stating the obvious, but you need to step back and unpack your assumptions—especially in the tough conversations, as this is where emotions can add to the mix of what may be misinterpreted.

Changing to behaviour-based language is a skill that you can learn, and it gets easier the more you practise. Practise so that it will start to become more automatic and you'll be able to switch it on and off as you need.

Guiding future behaviours

One of the reasons for having key conversations is to guide people on what you want them to do in the future. The more specific you are in your conversations about which behaviours you're looking for, the more likely it is that others will be able to repeat the behaviours you're after. For example, if someone in your team is showing a staff member a new system, you might reinforce them with a comment like, 'Oh, good work with the new employee—you did a great job'. This is nice, but it's not specific enough to allow that person to know what to repeat or do differently in the future. Your comments need to be more specific. The best thing you can do is describe the behaviour from a recent, real-life situation. For example, 'Love the work you did with Marcelo when you spent those two hours on Wednesday morning showing him how to navigate the STIP system. Being available for him to ask questions and trial the system with you was perfect'.

The detail in this feedback allows the individual to understand exactly which behaviour was appreciated. As a consequence, there is a strong likelihood they will perform the same task in the same way in the future. The specific detail you provide about behaviours allows people to repeat or stop a behaviour in the future.

Achieving clarity can take time, but it's worth it

Getting to the point where you are confident that both you and the other person have a shared understanding of expectations can sometimes feel laborious and time-consuming. It involves clarifying and checking that you're both on the same page. While this feels tedious, it's often an integral step in achieving success in key conversations. Time spent here clarifying expectations ultimately saves time in misunderstandings down the track such as the misunderstandings that occurred in the case study of Bernice and her manager.

Being able to achieve a greater level of clarity and understanding can sometimes involve asking the right questions. Questions such as, 'In your own words, can you tell me where we go from here?' or 'How do you interpret what we've been talking about?' or even 'What are the next steps?' will give you feedback about how the other person is interpreting the situation. They can help ensure that you're both on the same page, and help clarify any confusion or misinterpretation if you're not.

Managing up

Addressing traits and behaviours is a skill that can be used when managing up in order to get clear on what your boss expects from you. Listening for the times when you hear your boss talk in traits and responding with clarifying questions is an essential skill. For example, if your boss comes to you with a request to improve customer service (trait), you might seek clarification such as, 'What specific things do you want to see more of so that we can improve customer service?' or 'What does improved customer service look like to you?'

Taking the time to get clear on what your boss specifically wants more of, less of or done differently gives you a better chance of meeting these expectations. Remember that other people are not mind-readers: it's important to achieve clarity in your conversations, particularly the tough conversations, because clarity now will save you time in the long run.

Different definitions of traits: punctuality under the microscope

What punctuality (trait) means to you may depend on when you were born. To the veteran in the workforce, punctuality means being 15 minutes early: it doesn't mean on time, it means early. The Gen X person in the workplace is slap-bang on time, or one minute before, if that. The Gen Y employee can be somewhere between half an hour early and half an hour late, depending on how much they care about what they're attending. Obviously, this is a very broad classification, but it identifies the impact of the social make-up of the workforce, which can contribute to our understanding—or lack of understanding—of these traits. Punctuality doesn't have a single definition: its meaning depends on the person, their background, their make-up and even their age.

Depersonalising the conversation

Moving into behaviour-based language allows you to depersonalise a situation easily and talk about changing behaviours while being completely supportive of the individual. If you recall the case study on Tim, moving from talking about the trait of laziness to talking about specific behaviours helped to depersonalise this tough conversation. When we talk about traits, the conversation often gets very personal very quickly.

High-performance sports teams use the behaviour-based approach effectively. A team at the top of the ladder can get to the top of their field because they build a culture where they can be relentless on behaviour, but completely supportive of each other as a team. They can sit down and have a really robust discussion at the end of a game, target certain behaviours and say, 'We need to get better at that, but we know that we're capable of doing it'. Teams at the bottom of the ladder do not grasp this concept. When this is the case, providing feedback that is often laden with the description of traits starts to turn into fighting, bickering and poor morale.

High-performing teams in the workplace are those that can respect the individuals within the team while still being relentless in addressing key behaviours that need changing. As a result, individuals on the receiving end of this style of conversation feel supported as valued team members while also being clear on which behaviours they need to change. More workplaces would do well to grasp and embrace the behaviour-based approach.

Communication media

When it comes to having tough conversations and delivering tough messages there is a broad range of communication media that you can use: email, face-to-face or over the phone, group meeting or one-on-one.

Often we are asked which communication medium is best for the tough conversations. The simple answer is, 'All of them and none of them'. Each one of these communication media works exceptionally well given a certain set of circumstances, and each of them fails given a certain set of circumstances.

It's important to use a range of media. The bigger the message, the more media you use. When it comes to having the tough conversations, it's important to rely not only on face-to-face or just a phone call or just an email. Use all of them. Have a face-to-face conversation, ring the person up afterwards and also send an email confirming what you have spoken about, spreading these actions out over an appropriate time so that the key points remain front of mind. Use as many media as you can over a period of time in order to get your message across and allow opportunities for conversation.

Using just one medium (particularly if it is email) leaves the conversation open to assumptions, misinterpretation and miscommunication. Email is a poor way to communicate the tough conversations without using any other media. People fill the gaps with assumptions, and often these assumptions are incorrect and cause anger or frustration.

As we saw in the case study about Tim, even in a face-to-face conversation much is left unsaid, or said but not heard because the individual was focusing elsewhere. Whatever the message, if it's important (which the tough conversations always are) then it's important to have the conversation more than once and use as many media as is reasonable.

The power of words

The words that we use during the key conversations are integral to achieving success. In this section we will explore three key areas where your words can make a significant impact. They are:

- the 'live person rule'
- why don'ts don't work
- how using strengths-based language will revolutionise your conversations.

The 'live person rule'

When working with clients to decrease an undesired behaviour, many therapists use a guiding principle called the 'live person rule', which is the opposite of the 'dead person rule'. Sounds terrible, doesn't it? The dead person rule is not as horrific as it first sounds. It just means you should never ask someone to do something a dead person or inanimate object could do, such as not behaving. For example, you could say to a person, 'Don't walk out the door', and they could achieve the task by simply doing nothing. In fact, a glass on the table could also get the job done simply by being there—as could a pen, a bunch of fake flowers and also the main character in *Weekend at Bernie's*. To enact behaviour change we need to have people *doing* stuff rather than being passive and *not doing* stuff.

The aim is to use language in such a way that only a live person could complete the request. So instead of, 'Don't walk out the door', the request might be 'Stay in the room so that we can continue this conversation'. Participating in a conversation is not something a glass of water can do; it's something that only a live person can do. Pay attention to the conversations you hear in the office and around you, and listen for how often people make requests that a glass of water could carry out, and how often people make live person requests. The results may surprise you. Table 3.2 shows some examples of the poor requests you might hear in your office.

Table 3.2: examples of poor requests (dead person requests)

Situation or context	Instruction
Supervisor to trainee:	Don't come in late for work.
Manager to aggrieved employee:	I don't want you to take this the wrong way, but...
Manager to staff members at team meeting:	Don't come to these meetings without contributing.

Table 3.3 shows how these ineffective requests (dead person questions) can be rephrased using the live person rule.

Table 3.3: examples of dead person requests rephrased as live person requests

Dead person instruction	Live person rephrasing
Don't come in late for work.	Please be at work on time for a 9 am start.
I don't want you to take this the wrong way, but...	Let's make sure we're both on the same page.
Don't come to these meetings without contributing.	It is important that you contribute to these meetings.

Why don'ts don't work

In the vast majority of cases a dead person request starts with the words 'don't' or 'do not'. This approach can undermine the very result that you're trying to achieve and, when you're in a key conversation, can be totally derailing.

Unpacking further why don'ts don't work, let's look again at the simple request, 'Don't walk out the door' from the point of view of the listener. When the brain is examined under functional magnetic resonance imaging (fMRI) scans, we can see that it lights up in exactly the same areas regardless of whether there is a 'don't' at the start of the sentence or not. The word becomes just a small prefix on the front of what is actually the sentence. It seems that the word 'don't' is irrelevant to our brain.

This means that the request that has a 'don't' at the start becomes what we call a priming statement. Because 'walk out the door' is part of the request, we actually give people the armoury to carry out the act. It's almost like planting the seed for them.

'Don't walk out the door.' Their response? 'Oh, I hadn't thought of that.'

This is even more evident in statements beginning, 'I don't want you to take this the wrong way'. Seriously? This is a classic case of a priming statement. Whether they were going to or not, the other person is now on the lookout for ways to 'take it the wrong way'.

It's like saying, 'Don't think of a pink elephant', and all you can do is think of pink elephants. 'Don'ts' prime the listener for the very thing that you actually want them to steer clear of.

There are some other reasons why don'ts don't work. What's the largest part of the sentence? 'Walk out the door.' And the smallest? 'Don't.'

What's the last thing on the list? 'Walk out the door.' What's the first thing on the list? 'Don't.'

The primacy and recency effect is strong in our memory. Recency is more powerful in our memory: the things that we hear last in a series or a list are the things that we remember best. The fact that the most important part of the sentence is the last (or most recent) part is another reason the statement, 'Don't walk out the door' doesn't work.

It's important to rephrase your 'don't' statements. Instead of the 'don'ts' and 'do not's', change your language into action-based requests.

You can see this in action in public places such as parks. Over the past 15 to 20 years there has been a massive change in the language used on signs. Years ago signs at the local park carried statements such as 'Don't walk on the grass'. Local councils have realised that 'don'ts' don't work and the signs now express specific requests for desired behaviour, such as 'Keep to the footpath'.

Focus on strengths

Marcus Buckingham, international author and speaker on strengths, is one of a number of people leading a revolution to get people to focus more on our areas of strength than on improving our areas of weakness. We believe you can also apply this philosophy to your language. The reality is that if you operate within a weakness-based vocabulary, your chances of achieving results in the tough stuff are severely hindered. Consider table 3.4, which shows unhelpful traits (in the left-hand column) and some selected strengths (in the right-hand column) that are contained within the unhelpful trait.

Table 3.4: taking unhelpful traits and finding strengths within them

Unhelpful trait	Strengths contained within the trait
whingeing	identifies problems
stubborn	steadfast or determined
lazy	calm, relaxed or laid-back
cynical	realistic or worldly
abrupt	direct
uncaring	logical
aggressive	forthright or passionate
withdrawn	compliant or introverted
opinionated	ideas person or contributor
arrogant	confident
tactless	direct or up-front
interfering	inquisitive
sceptical	thorough
argumentative	facilitates debate
loud	extroverted

If you talk about the unhelpful traits in a tough-stuff conversation of any kind, we believe it will derail your efforts at best and completely disable them at worst. Success in the conversation lies in the right-hand column: you have to move the conversation towards the strengths, and in turn the behaviours, you wish to see.

For example, let's say we decide to have a conversation with an employee. First, the poor way: 'So I think it's time we had a conversation. I want to talk to you about being arrogant'. How's that going to go? That conversation is heading south fast. The naming of an unhelpful trait will crush the chance of a productive conversation.

Now let's try refocusing from the unhelpful trait to a strengths-based language approach. If you focus on the strengths contained in the trait of arrogance, you paint a different picture yet remain on the same topic. What we might focus on is confidence. We know that one of the great strengths of any arrogant person is that they're confident. Sometimes it's just overblown. So let's try starting the conversation using the strengths approach.

'I'd like to have a chat to you about your confidence. One of your strengths is you're a confident guy, but there are times that confidence can be a little overbearing or misplaced. Let me give you an example ...'. It's a different conversation about the same topic. It works and provides us with a platform to move into behavioural language, which will make this situation even more productive.

You may not yet be convinced. 'Isn't it drawing a long bow?' you may question. 'If they're arrogant, then shouldn't they just be called that?'

We believe you can label people with these left-hand columns and be 100 per cent right. But you can also be 100 per cent unhappy with the result of the key conversation, and with your relationship with this person. Sometimes you have to give up your sense of 'being right' to be happy. Talk to someone about being arrogant and they will get defensive; talk to the person about being confident and they are more likely to hear what you're saying.

Strip back your message

With the advent of Twitter and status updates on Facebook, we are being asked to exercise the skill of stripping back our message to the core (to 140 characters or less, in fact). We think this is a good skill to learn, particularly if you are in a leadership role. Imagine if your manager or CEO came along to your next meeting and was able to clearly explain the vision, strategy and purpose of the organisation in 140 characters (or less). What would that be like?

There's a saying that 'the most important thing is to know the most important thing'. How many people in your team and your organisation know what the most important thing they need to do is? If you're a manager and a leader then you need to ask yourself the following questions:

- What is the most important point I need to get across at the moment?
- What is the most important goal I need my staff to be striving towards?
- What is the core intent behind our actions as a team?

Dan Heath and Chip Heath, prolific writers and columnists for the magazine *Fast Company*, have written a brilliant book called *Made to Stick*. Their book talks about having a message, idea and strategy that is 'sticky' — one that stays with people for a long time.

Too often we feel like we have to add more to our message, idea or strategy so that it can be made clear to others. In fact, stripping back your message to the core is more important. Take the time to think about your core vision, goal, idea and strategy, and how you can communicate this to your staff and your customers in 140 characters (or less). And if you're stuck, then take the time to read *Made to Stick*.

Conclusion

Generally speaking, we do most of our communication through three key areas: the words we write, the words we say and our body language. This chapter has given you a series of tools to help you communicate in the first two areas. The third, non-verbal communication, is discussed in chapter 4.

It's time to lead a revolution. Let's get rid of the fluffy language. Let's have trust that the people we talk to will appreciate clarity and conciseness in a conversation, and let's be more direct about how we communicate with each other. We get so wrapped up in trying to soften things that we make the conversation grey when black and white would be much better.

Darren's insights

I want to talk about love. No, it is not Valentine's Day, and I am acutely aware of the work context of this book. That being said, I believe love has a real business case at work. I'm talking about love in the form of trust.

The work I do with executives comes from a place of trusting them and trusting myself to be able to handle the tough conversations. When I work with executives I'm like a sculptor with a block of granite. I use really big tools: I work on the tough cases and I promise I will give it to them straight. This comes from a place of compassion and wanting to see others grow and develop. I love to work with people who don't mind the challenge. I have faith in a straight message because I know intimately that sometimes the only way to make a big step or a leap ahead is to face some of the tough stuff. I know that sometimes they are going to hurt and that it will really shake them up. I also know and have trust that they're going to get through it. Trust your staff enough to tell them straight, without withholding information. That's a deep, positive regard for another—that's love.

Alison's insights

Too often in the key conversations there are lots of words used but not much is actually said. Having worked closely in a clinical setting with individuals who suffer from depression, anxiety and other mental-health problems, I am continually amazed about two things: how rarely the issues of the heart are ever given a voice; and how much people hold onto small statements, sometimes for years. I believe the same happens in the workplace and that it causes much anxiety, heartache and isolation.

Imagine a workplace where individuals are encouraged to discuss what is at the heart of an interpersonal issue; a workplace where small statements that currently play on your mind are discussed openly and explained rather than left to fester; a workplace where people get to the point quickly. Removing the fluff, getting down to practical actions and focusing on strengths are the starting point to making this a reality.

Sean's insights

I apply a fundamental principle, born of experience: support the person, challenge the behaviour.

What I have noticed is that some people get defensive more easily, or are in a more vulnerable state, such that you need to spend more time in support mode to break down barriers to communication before you can challenge them. Other people have more robust self-esteem, or have fewer stressors at that time in life, and will get bored if you don't quickly get onto a bit of challenge in your feedback. You have to be discerning about when to support and when to challenge.

Once you have determined which feedback a person needs at that moment—more support or more challenge—you have the tools for how to provide support and challenge. To support a person, convert negative trait language into strengths-based language, and linger in this context when you feel they are in a more vulnerable state. To challenge someone's behaviour, convert the negative trait labels into detailed behavioural descriptions of things that need to change.

Chapter summary

- Misinterpretations and misunderstandings are all too common in key conversations because individuals are not clear with their language.

- Depersonalise a tough conversation by addressing specific behaviours rather than talking in terms of traits (which are more easily misinterpreted due to individuals having different definitions of common words).

- A trait is a label for a set of behaviours, and a behaviour is something that is directly observable.

- Break down the behaviours that make up a trait and focus the tough conversation on changing the behaviours.

- The more important the message the more communication media you need to use.

- Avoid the 'dead person rule' and remember that 'don'ts' don't work. Instead, clearly articulate the desired behaviour.

- Focus on using strengths-based language.

When in doubt,
PEOPLE TRUST
BODY
LANGUAGE
MORE THAN
WORDS.

4

DEALING WITH THE UNSAID STUFF

Ensuring maximum leverage from your non-verbal communication

We have all heard the statistics about how much of our communication is non-verbal. Some researchers say that up to 90 per cent of communication is non-verbal. Regardless of the validity and reliability of these statistics, two things are certain: we absolutely communicate with others without speaking, and non-verbal communication makes a huge difference to how a message is both sent and received.

The correct use of non-verbal communication techniques is a game-changer in tough-stuff conversations. We can achieve great levels of clarity through our language; there is little doubt that an array of well-positioned phrases and key words will get us better outcomes in the key conversations. But we can undo all of this with an incorrect or inopportune use of our eyes, hands or body posture at a critical point. Non-verbal communication is like baker's yeast: all of the base ingredients can be present, but the end product can rise to great heights or fall flat if the non-verbal component is left out of the mix.

Non-verbal communication

Human beings have an incredible capacity to identify and gauge situations based on reading non-verbal communication and body language. We know that a large percentage of our communication happens non-verbally, and yet very few of us are conscious of how our body language affects a conversation.

The world's pre-eminent non-verbal specialist is, we believe, Michael Grinder. Having conducted more than four decades of specialised research into behavioural dynamics in and around education, and more than 6000 individual classroom observations of teachers' non-verbal communication, Michael is quite simply 'the man' when it comes to understanding how to establish the difference between using non-verbal communication effectively and using it ineffectively. We strongly encourage you to visit his website at www. michaelgrinder.com and attend one of his workshops or read one of his books. Without question it will change how you communicate with others—for the better.

Approachable versus credible

Our hands are incredibly powerful in our spoken conversation for a couple of reasons, and those reasons are mainly around our voice control. Why are we talking about non-verbal communication techniques, when we are about to talk about voice tones? The fact is that our hands and our head (non-verbal) drive the type of voice tone we use (verbal). Not only is it fascinating, it has a huge impact on how you deliver a key message.

When we speak with our hands up (particularly coupled with a moving or bobbing head), our voice tends to finish on an upwards inflection and the result is a bouncy voice pattern. This is called an 'approachable' voice pattern. It's the voice pattern we use when building rapport or when meeting someone for the first time. It's a 'hey-there-nice-to-meet-you' voice pattern that is very likeable. Next time you do a bit of people-watching, take note.

When our hands are down and our head stays still and back on our shoulders, we deliver a different voice pattern: the 'credible' voice pattern. Two things happen when the credible voice pattern is engaged: our voice tone dips at the end of sentences, and we tend to pause more often and breathe more deeply. This produces a serious, measured voice pattern that is eminently believable. In fact, when the credible voice pattern is used effectively you can be talking nonsense and people still want to believe you!

A useful analogy when considering approachable and credible voice patterns is taking a trip on a plane. The pilot uses the credible voice tone: 'This is your captain speaking', whereas the cabin staff use an approachable voice tone: 'We hope you have a pleasant flight'. It would be disconcerting if the two were swapped, wouldn't it? We don't care too much if the pilot is a people person—we just want to know everything is under control. On the other hand, we want the cabin staff to be engaging and approachable rather than abrupt and serious.

According to Grinder, a lot of men struggle with approachability because they traditionally tend to talk with their hands down. Women, on the other hand, can sometimes struggle for credibility. This is because most women naturally use a facing-up hand position when they are talking, so they tend to talk approachably. It is easy to see how this can be a double-edged sword. Sometimes you are seen as too harsh (using credible instead of approachable), while at other times you may be viewed as flaky (using approachable when credible was needed).

Let's look at an example of voice tones at work. Have you ever dealt with someone on the phone over a period of time, and finally you meet them face to face and say, 'You are so different from what I expected!'? Generally speaking, we use credible voice tone while on the phone. Our hands are down (on the computer or writing) and our head is still (it has to be because we're on the phone), so we end up using a credible voice tone. Then, when we finally meet, we tend to use an approachable tone because that's natural when first meeting or greeting someone. This is why someone can seem so different when we change from phone to face-to-face communication.

When considering the use of approachable-versus-credible voice patterns in the tough-stuff conversations, assess whether your primary focus is on being taken seriously—if so, use the credible voice pattern—or on building rapport, in which case you should use the approachable voice pattern.

Making your point

In chapter 3 we looked in detail at how to depersonalise tough-stuff conversations by using behaviour-based language rather than trait-based language—this works incredibly well to help you separate the person from the behaviour, while achieving clarity. When this strategy is used alongside the correct non-verbal patterns, however, your success moves to a whole new level.

In delivering our Dealing with the Tough Stuff training program to thousands of people across Australia and North America, we educate participants on the effect of our non-verbal communication methods on personalising and depersonalising a conversation. Most people have an *a-ha* moment. Usually that's for three reasons:

- It just makes sense.
- We realise we have been educated the wrong way.
- It isn't difficult to remedy.

A closer examination of non-verbal communication, in particular where we *direct* our conversation, reveals four points of communication that we use every day. Primarily driven by the direction of our eyes, these four points have a considerable impact on how verbal messages are sent and received. Let's look at each of them in detail.

One-point communication

One-point communication is typically when our eyes look downwards into our personal space. This form of communication usually accompanies reflective practice: for example, when we say, 'The other day I was thinking to myself' we almost always drop our eyes and look into our personal space.

One-point communication serves us well for clearing the slate — that is, moving from closing off one section of information to starting the next. Next time you watch a television newsreader, observe how they look down at one point between news stories.

One-point communication is a very effective strategy for leading staff members to reflect on their actions. In using one-point communication, we do not enforce personal judgement, but when role-modelled effectively, one-point communication allows the other person to reflect on themselves.

Two-point communication

Two-point communication is characterised (particularly in the Western world) by the use of direct eye contact. It should not be simply defined as eye contact alone, though. A better definition would be 'looking into someone else's space'. In most Western workplace cultures two-point communication takes place as an eye-contact scenario. If you are having conversations with people from certain cultures, such as some Indigenous Australian and some Asian cultures, you may not find as much direct eye contact, owing to cultural norms, but two-point communication is still taking place. Regardless of the cultural role of direct or indirect eye contact, two-point communication is looking into another's space.

Two-point communication is the most personal communication, and it is mostly used for positive exchange. Yet we tend to overuse two-point communication, especially when we are having the tough-stuff conversations. In fact we've been taught to look the person in the eye and deliver our message. And yet, given the rapport nature of this point of communication, this is how tough conversations become personalised very quickly.

Three-point communication

Three-point communication is where the speaker and the listener both 'share' an independent visual medium. For example, they both look at a whiteboard, or they both look at the agenda for the team meeting. By doing this, they do not look into each other's space (eye contact or two-point communication), but use a shared space to conduct the conversation.

Three-point communication helps us to talk about 'it' rather than talk about 'you', and directs the conversation towards a process, which depersonalises the conversation.

Four-point communication

When we use four-point communication we're referring to something that is not present. In four-point communication our eyes usually look up-and-out, or up-and-behind, signalling something outside of the space that we're currently in, off into the distance. For example, if we were to mention how great it would be to double our profits next year, we would use four-point communication because what you hope for hasn't been achieved yet.

The game-changer

'I don't know why they took it so personally? It was just a work conversation ...'

If you have ever uttered this phrase, then we suggest you probably communicated the information using a two-point communication process, where you were giving negative or challenging feedback and probably using direct eye contact.

By using two-point communication, or direct eye contact—the most personal communication medium—the person on the receiving end has no other way to take the message than personally!

Here's the problem. We were taught, 'Look them in the eye: it shows them you're serious, it's respectful'. And, 'If you can't look them in the eye, then you're lying' or, worse still, 'you're a coward'. There are many other social rules that are not founded on science or even on simple cause and effect.

Using two-point communication as your dominant medium when communicating the tough stuff is likely to lead to escalated conflict or personal anguish.

Direct eye contact in tough conversations simply doesn't work. View the cause and effect and it is easy to leave it behind and move to a much better form of communication.

Using three-point communication is the better alternative for tough-stuff conversations.

The single greatest effect that using the three-point method in the tough stuff achieves is creating a sense of distance from the issue. Both the speaker and the listener are allowed to refer to the problem rather than the person. It's incredibly powerful in achieving behaviour change, which is the aim of the tough-stuff conversation.

Direct eye contact
IS OUR FASTEST WAY TO
BUILD TRUST
AND MAKE THINGS
PERSONAL;
use it wisely.

When it comes to addressing the tough stuff at work, here's the golden rule: have more of the tough-stuff conversations using three-point communication and fewer using the two-point.

We understand that this can be enormously challenging. For some readers our suggestions will compete with a lifetime of learnt behaviour, but sometimes we can get very good at something that actually doesn't serve us well.

The most comfortable place for a tough-stuff conversation to take place is in the three-point medium because it allows you to stay calm — and it allows the other party to stay calm as well. Both are critical states to stay in, in order to achieve an effective outcome.

Watch the contamination

Whenever we're conducting a tough-stuff conversation, we're at risk of contaminating a space — of corrupting it by contact or association. There's always an element of infecting a space when we have less-than-great conversations. Interestingly, the contaminated space can be both physical and personal at the same time. That means you have a choice: which space do you choose to contaminate?

If you use two-point communication, you contaminate the personal space. If you have eyeballed someone while giving negative feedback, the result is usually people walking down hallways trying not to look each other in the eye because the personal space has been contaminated by two-point, and therefore unsatisfactory, tough-stuff conversations. If you have given someone both barrels in your office, they may avoid coming into your office in the future — they will stand in the hallway beyond your door, but they won't step in. It's because you have contaminated the space.

If you use three-point communication, you contaminate only the shared visual space, so three-point is the best place to conduct the conversation.

Grounded in science

Our confidence in three-point communication being a real game-changer is not based simply on our own observations and teachings, nor is it based on four decades of study by Michael Grinder. Its value is also backed by science.

When we use two-point communication, we engage our emotional brain more rapidly, and as a direct result our long-term memory storage also. These bodily responses are fantastic for positive conversations, but they are not productive for the tough-stuff conversations. We all want to be remembered for the right reasons, not the wrong ones.

Studies show that direct eye contact automatically raises our heart rate and our metabolism. Our pupils dilate, our temperature rises and our cortisol (stress hormone) levels rise. There is a lot of chaos starting in our bodies when eye contact takes place.

What is the one thing we look for when leading a conversation that's crucial? The ability to stay calm: three-point communication helps you (and the other person) stay calm.

Conclusion

Non-verbal communication can strengthen or prevent even the best theory from being practised successfully. Conversely, when you use your eyes, body and hands consciously you can take the same theory and get outstanding results. Yet even with the promise of extraordinary results, many people ignore working on their non-verbal patterns in favour of their existing behavioural patterns. Changing the way you use your non-verbal patterns with others will feel strange. For some readers it may go against decades of learnt behaviour. Our request to you is to examine whether your current non-verbal pattern usage is getting you the best possible results. If not, it's time for a change. When you couple the correct non-verbal means of communication with the learning from the rest of this book, your success rate in dealing with the tough stuff will be incredibly high—you will become a leader worth following.

Darren's insights

When I was studying psychology at university I was in awe of Carl Rogers and his approach to therapy, the concept of unconditional positive regard. Basically, this says you should be open and supportive of the client and use lots of eye contact to let them know you're there for them all the way.

Unconditional positive regard (and the non-verbal process attached to it) actually requires a couple of conditions for it to work effectively: unlimited time and access. One visit will rarely, if ever, achieve success. I don't know any manager who has unlimited time and access, so unconditional positive regard isn't going to work. I still love Rogers's approach—for its positive exchanges—but for the busy manager who needs to have a direct conversation and not follow it up with 10 visits, three-point communication is your best friend at work.

Alison's insights

When it comes to talking about non-verbal communication, there are key differences between men and women. According to the Body Language Expert at www.bodylanguageexpert.co.uk, women tend to make more eye contact than men. This may be related to women's tendency to strive for emotional connection when communicating. It's important that women are aware of this tendency when they step into three-point communication.

The initial feedback from managers about three-point communication is that not using eye contact to connect with others feels disrespectful. It's important to let go of this belief as quickly as possible. Using three-point communication to discuss tough feedback is incredibly respectful and allows you to reserve eye contact for positive connection and engagement. If you're a woman struggling with this approach, recognise your natural tendency to use eye contact, and remember that connection and respect are born of supporting people to change their behaviours towards success. Three-point communication is an effective tool to this end.

Sean's insights

When I was teaching three-point communication recently, a manager in the audience said, 'I thought we are supposed to build relationships by engaging with people. Aren't you disengaging from your audience when you talk in the third-point?'. My answer was, 'Yes—and creating a subtle level of disengagement when you're having a tough-stuff conversation is the point of the exercise'. Engaging people in the second-point with negative or critical feedback prompts them to put up defensive walls. They may look like they're listening to your feedback as they return your gaze, but internally they have completely disengaged, and any solution you provide will fall on deaf ears.

Use three-point communication to create just enough disengagement so that listeners won't get defensive. Invite them to view the problematic behaviour as a behaviour that can be changed, rather than a character flaw that can't.

Chapter summary

- Watch and listen for the use of 'credible' versus 'approachable' voice patterns in your workplace. Who uses them effectively?

- Become a people watcher: tune into others using the four points of communication.

- Explain the difference between two-point and three-point communication to another person. The best form of learning is teaching.

- Use three-point communication more often, particularly in group settings. You will see that people open up as a result.

- Examine your propensity to use two-point communication in dealing with the tough stuff. Have you been schooled the wrong way?

- Save the two-point method of communication for positive interactions. Try a week of using three-point communication in all conversations that are less than positive.

- Help others help themselves. When you're in a conversation with your boss, ensure you create a three-point space, even if they don't. Until you get them to read this book they won't know any better.

The global shift towards
REMOTE WORKERS
opens up
**EXCITING
OPPORTUNITIES**
and also
**SIGNIFICANT
CHALLENGES,**
especially for
KEY
CONVERSATIONS.

5

DEALING WITH THE REMOTE STUFF

Having the key conversations when geography is an issue

It seems like only yesterday it was the norm to lead a team of people at work under one roof. Yet, in 2016 the number of workers operating virtually, or remotely, is increasing at an unprecedented rate as technology provides platforms for touch points that can feel almost as if everyone is in the same location. Despite many business models embracing the new world model of outsourcing and remote-based staff, it's a different work culture from the one built under one roof, a culture with both benefits and obstacles for the modern work team. No matter how advanced our technology becomes, we acknowledge that it will always provide a significant challenge when it comes to tough-stuff conversations.

According to recent reports, within a few years more than 1.3 billion people will work virtually—that is, through rich electronic connections from sites of their choosing. Along with this global shift will come exciting opportunities and also significant challenges, especially for the key conversations that those managing and leading this workforce will need to possess.

Before we give you principles and areas to be mindful of when tackling the tough stuff with remote staff, let's first look at the opportunities that exist now and into the future.

Find the best, don't choose from the rest

The war for talent just got a whole lot bigger. Rather than skirmishes within small local areas, the frontline battle is already taking place across countless countries because of the most spectacularly disruptive force of modern times: the internet.

With the revolution swamping workplaces like a veritable digital tsunami, the necessity to source people from your local area has become a yoke removed from many organisational recruitment and development strategies.

The concept of selecting the biggest and best goldfish from your small geographical pond is, in many cases, redundant; an ocean of talent has become available to the organisations that embrace a remote-based staffing mindset.

Even big, mature national and multinational businesses are forging a new path for team structures these days. In the past, teams were often built around the regularity of face-to-face contact, rather than best fit for the organisational strategy. As a consequence, teams were put together as 'all rounders,' rather than as experts with specific complementary talents. Local teams had to resemble the basic offerings from the whole business, trying to be a one-stop shop at the risk of doing it poorly. This has changed considerably: many teams within large organisations are located across the globe, connecting and delivering specific outcomes in their deep expertise areas.

Whether you're a small business, fast-start company in pre-launch mode, or a mature organisation with thousands of employees, the availability of brilliant people has never been better.

Find flexibility or narrow your choices

Nestled alongside remote-based teams as a major workplace shift in recent years is the advent of flexible work practices. What used to be a groovy Silicon Valley trademark—ditch the 9-to-5—has become practically a basic workplace right: tailored work hours, whether for the work-from-home parent; the overseas or interstate team member; or the high-talent, lifestyle-focused next-gen. Once again, such shifting workforce practices help broaden the talent pool as well as leverage the strengths of your existing staff

The other growth in how we work is the pool of people who are located in a similar vicinity but who are out in the field much more, resulting in a loss of connection with the person whose desk may be only metres away. Because technology allows for regular 'check-ins' at any time, anywhere, the face-to-face connections have been significantly reduced. While it's certainly a challenge to have both a remote-based team and also one that works incredibly varied work hours, it does give the opportunity for something quite special. Work can be done while you're sleeping!

This all bodes well when work is going great, but how do you address key issues with staff when it may be a week before you see them, or when the tyranny of distance makes it hard for you to bring it up?

Key challenges for leading a remote team

While opening the doors to a more global and connected workforce brings with it great opportunity, when it comes to having the tough conversations in remote teams there are key challenges. The only way to address these challenges is through understanding their impact and then setting up guiding principles for leading remote teams.

Absence of contact

The most obvious challenge facing cultures with remote team members is the decrease in opportunity for people to come together in person and simply spend time with each other. With a richness of verbal and non-verbal language present during direct contact, it still is, and always will be, the communication medium through which people build trust most quickly and form the deepest relationships.

No matter how advanced our technology becomes, it's difficult to envisage workplaces developing a platform that will provide authentic, informal human touch points that match those which happen at the water cooler or in the tea-room. While they could seem trivial at times, these non-transactional exchanges remain critical for group dynamics and function.

The smallest touch

In addition to the richness of language modalities, the virtual world has yet to replicate another crucial medium of connection: physical touch. Touch still matters for relationships. Sure, we can form relationships with people we've never met, but in rapid-change environments where challenges present themselves, sometimes like hailstorms, the closeness of your team's bonds will be the true shelter from any tempest. The fastest and deepest way we build these strong bonds? Through physical contact. A handshake here, a high-five there. The reassuring hand on someone's arm when they're struggling, or maybe even a hug when they need it the most. While we can set up expert teams in any area and in any time zone, we will miss something critically important in deeply connected relationships of any kind: the unspoken trust that develops from physical contact.

Later in this chapter we'll explore the neuroscience behind why deep connection is so important, and what you need to do on the very occasional times when you do actually spend time with others in the same space.

The relationship is what matters

With this zeitgeist of location and time independence sweeping every industry in every country, new challenges exist continually in task assignment, accountability and reporting. There is an array of software options (at the time of writing these include Asana, Trello, Basecamp and Slack) to provide structure and clarity of duties, yet few of these produce the number-one driver of discretionary effort for an employee: the quality of the relationship between an employee and their direct manager.

Take time to think about the managers you've worked for in the past — the person who took time to cultivate a relationship with you was most likely the manager for whom you did that bit extra. Conversely, most people have had the experience of working for a manager who wasn't emotionally invested. As a result, you may have hesitated investing the extra effort. Sure, you may have produced the occasional above-average effort, but your default was more likely to be middle-of-the-road, at best, and bare minimum, at worst.

Five guiding principles for communicating remotely

Without the richness of face-to-face social interaction in remote teams, the building of the critical manager–report relationship is more difficult, but certainly not beyond us. To ensure we create a trusted, inspiring and productive relationship, there are some key principles we need to follow when using remote communications.

Do the extras on personal connection

The first principle is about over-empathising; that is, doing more than you think is necessary to get into the other person's world. Get into their shoes, show care and interest and connect with their experience. Understand their position for your work objectives and also get interested in the person with whom you are connecting, not just the worker. With remote communication, it's more important than ever to put effort into authentic personal connection, yet it's easier than ever to avoid it completely. When you don't have to walk past someone in the hall or the lunch room and aren't required to engage in day-to-day social graces, it's easy to become lazy about personal effort. Maybe you plan to be more personable, but pressure is on and time is tight, so you postpone your personal connection efforts to a chat when you'll have more time. Don't put off the personal stuff! In fact, it's even more important to overload the personal in the early days of remote communication; building a strong foundation of rapport will serve you well for those future moments when you only have time for a brief transactional chat. Furthermore, choose the most personal medium you can: go for a video chat rather than the phone, or send a detailed email rather than a cryptic text.

Keep it real

The second principle—virtual reality—means trying to get something as close to the real thing as possible. It can be easy to treat remote conversations differently from other conversations. They're not as 'real' so we may let a few things slide. Just because there's an ocean or an ethernet cable between you and the person at the other end of the line, doesn't mean you should drop the important bits of a face-to-face conversation. Undivided attention, respect, active listening, engagement: all of these are still crucial. But, with remote communication there's an increased opportunity for unchecked external distractions. So, you need to do the little things we normally do that facilitate good face-to-face interactions: turn off the phone, shut down the web browser (unless you're googling something relevant to the conversation), update Facebook later, turn off email and its notifications, and get present to the person in front of you! If you're the person who is remote and at home, have a shower and put on a work shirt—no hanging out in your PJs (even if it's not a video conference). You'll feel sharper and communicate more professionally. If it's a formal conversation or meeting, set up an agenda and stick to time frames.

Continually monitor and navigate bias

The third guiding principle for communicating remotely involves avoiding bias. One of the biggest challenges with remote communication is that, with a greater absence of typical communication cues such as body language, facial expressions (including emotional micro-expressions), tone, projection, emphases and spatial orientation of body position, we have a lot of blank space around words, obscuring the communicator's intention, meaning and emotional state (see figure 5.1). This blank space increases significantly as we go to less personal and briefer forms of communication such as email and texting. Without sufficient cues, receivers of the communication will fill in the blank space, interpreting the message through a biased lens based on their own emotional states, intentions and meaning, potentially creating significantly altered messaging and unnecessary tough stuff. When you're delivering the communication, be careful not to assume that your intention, meaning and emotional tone are clear; similarly to the personal stuff, err on the side of providing extra clarity. If you're receiving the communication, constantly challenge yourself to see beyond your lens of interpretation, and seek clarity and reassurance of the communicator's intention, meaning and emotions.

Figure 5.1: communication medium vs interpretation bias

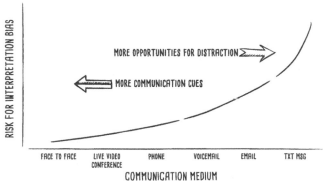

Use your tough-stuff skills

The fourth principle is to keep practising the tough-stuff skills outlined in the other chapters of this book, and make sure there's effective training and development on these crucial human skills for all involved. Bring all of your tough-stuff skills into the conversation. Find innovative ways to deliver a remote tough-stuff conversation using Michael Grinder's three-point communication (for example, have them draw a model that you talk through, or email them a document you can discuss over the phone). Make sure your emails are written in 'behaviour-versus-trait' language, and practise exploring the antecedents from the ABC model, even in a texting exchange.

Leverage technology BIG TIME!

The final principle entails using the best technology possible to deliver on principles one to four wherever you can: to facilitate personal connection, simulate real face-to-face conversations, navigate interpretation biases and implement the tough-stuff skills. However, be wary of both user and technology limitations—it's no good using the latest virtual-reality video conferencing technology if it takes 30 minutes of your meeting time to set up and connect, or if poor bandwidth at one end creates long pauses and dropouts. Sometimes the good old landline connection serves you best!

Get to know which platforms perform best for your circumstances; for example, maybe it's Skype for one-on-ones, Google Hangouts for informal group conversations or the group discussion forum on Basecamp for remote group problem solving. And, where you can, look to leverage the digital versions of analogue communication mediums, as you would in any face-to-face meeting. For example, if you like to create visuals and draw models in a meeting using a whiteboard, then get a digital whiteboard or sketch pad (and learn how to use it well before you bring it to the online conversation!). If you like to move around the room when you talk, make sure your video camera has a wide-enough angle lens, and ensure you stay in frame in order to capture the rich body language that comes with your movement. Invest in a high-quality microphone and headset to deliver the best audio possible. And, wherever you can, upskill on user technology capability—both your own and your team's. (Ever been frustrated trying to troubleshoot a tech glitch on social media with Mum? Upskilling is worth the investment!)

If you embed these guidelines into your general approach to the remote stuff, you'll be far ahead of the game.

The process

If you want to go one step further into the detail of how to go about any single remote conversation, we know it helps to have a method for the madness, so we've created a blow-by-blow process to follow for delivering your next remote tough-stuff conversation: prepare, engage, frame, focus, explore, conclude and plan.

Prepare: be ready in advance

It ain't rocket science (and we would say the same thing for the face-to-face tough-stuff conversations), but good preparation sets you up for success. We know it can be easy to treat remote conversations with less care, particularly the non-video kind, because of the decreased accountability that comes with decreased visibility. However, what are you in your role for? To get stuff done or to get away with not doing stuff? It's tough to speak off the cuff for the tough stuff—script it out to get it out! If it's complex, create an outline, agenda, objectives and resolutions, all within a time frame. If it feels awkward, practise delivering to a mirror until it comes out smoothly: you may be surprised at how good a communicator you can be when you prepare well!

Engage: rapport first

Following the first principle on pages 77–78 for communicating remotely, make sure you emphasise the personal stuff right up front. Time pressures may drive you to dispense with the rapport stuff and go straight to the detailed content, but if you haven't captured your audience, you're wasting your time anyway. It's better to have a person leaning forward, buying in and integrating one important piece of feedback than a person resisting 10 pieces of what you deem to be important information. Build rapport at every opportunity—it's always a step in the right direction.

Frame: set the scene with context and purpose

If you want to capture your audience, give them direction at the outset. Make sure people know what you're going to talk about and why before you get too far into it. Get alignment and buy-in early on rather than dealing with irrelevant tangents down the track.

Focus: get to the point

Once you've connected personally and framed the conversation, get right into the concise feedback. Nail your core take-homes early in the conversation and keep it simple. If you have 10 points of feedback to give them, just deliver the top three today (you'll get to the other seven in good time).

Explore: get input on others' perspectives

Give people time and your attention to provide their side of the story. Make it safe by creating an environment of non-judgemental observation. Explicitly state you're not there to judge what they have to say, only to understand so you can problem-solve with them more effectively.

Conclude: close the loop—resolve issues and answer questions

When you have time and space between important conversations, which you do with a remote team member, you don't want to leave crucial issues unresolved until the next scheduled touch point. This can leave them vulnerable to festering, creating unnecessary resentment and conflict (it's like the saying, 'the secret to a happy marriage is not to go to bed angry'). Make sure you and your staff member have addressed the key questions and created a resolution to or an action plan for the pressing issues before you finish the conversation.

Plan: commit to connection — schedule the next meeting before you hang up

We know that a lack of presence decreases accountability, and the moment you hang up it's 'out of sight, out of mind', so it's crucial to keep remote communication frequent, regular and responsive (particularly if there are any unresolved issues). The easiest way to do that is to end each remote chat with a confirmed date for connecting again, particularly if there are ongoing issues to resolve (they aren't just going to go away because the person is far away).

* * *

When it gets tough, don't fall into the trap of taking the easy option. If it's a tough conversation, look for your best option.

By following these guidelines and this process you'll not only avoid some of the biggest mistakes managers make when leading teams that aren't co-located, but you'll ensure you follow a process that works.

It's more than a transaction

While principles help to guide us, sometimes numbers can help us to balance our connections to ensure we're getting optimal leverage.

What's your ratio?

Each day we have numerous interactions with our colleagues, our team, our staff and our customers. Thinking about the types of interactions that you have with each of these groups, it's worth considering what your ratio is between positive and negative interactions. How many times do you give a positive comment as opposed to a negative comment?

Far too often when we're separated by distance we default to transactional communication: When I want something, I ring. When you need something, you text. We're both busy, so let's not waste each other's time with meaningless 'chit-chat' next time we're on Skype. Oh, and the teleconference... let's stick to an incredibly tight agenda ...' And all of that, as well meaning as it seems, can be a problem.

While transactional communication also happens in both the remote and co-located office environments, the chance of sociable communication occurring—asking how each other's day is, checking in on wellbeing, having a laugh together—is much more likely in an office environment. And while it seems trivial, this unintended sociability is an important factor for engendering trust and building functional relationships.

Transactional relationships in typical workplaces are more likely to favour critique—not necessarily belittlement or condescension, but constructive feedback for improved effort. Nonetheless, no matter how well intended the critique is, it's still not reinforcement or reward, creating an unfavourable imbalance on the negative.

In 2005, psychologist Marcial Losada uncovered an important ratio that provides us with some interesting reflection. Studying a range of relationship dynamics, Losada discovered a minimal ratio of approximately 3:1 exists between the positive and negative human interactions required for relationships to flourish.

In easy–speak, that means if in your relationship you're having fewer than three positive exchanges (such as reinforcement or praise) for every negative exchange (such as critique), you're on the pathway to dysfunction.

According to Losada, while 2.9013 is the minimal ratio required to lift teams and relationships above dysfunction, dysfunction also occurs when the ratio of positive to negative exceeds 11:1. In other words, when there is too much honey, people drown in it! It's not simply the absence of reinforcement that can harm a relationship's function, it's also the absence of critique. Having the right balance is essential.

The optimal ratio used by high-performing teams sits between 5:1 and 6:1, wherein the majority of communication is positive in its delivery. Nevertheless, communication in high-performing teams still drives accountability and provides the necessary critical feedback.

Like all populist social theories, Losada's work has and will be challenged, particularly around the validity of optimal ratios of positive to negative communication. However, at face value his model remains extremely useful for the manager leading remote employees.

So before you read on, we want you to consider the following question. Where is your ratio currently sitting? Better still, if you have a pen and paper, follow these two steps:

- Write down the names of all your direct reports.

- Give an approximate positive–negative feedback ratio for each person.

Invariably, you'll find the ratios are lower for direct reports with whom you are experiencing conflict. It's imperative to create positive exchanges with your tough customers in order to reverse such relationships from descending into chronic dysfunction, which is extremely difficult to undo.

With staff that aren't co-located, you may also see the ratios trending towards the skinny side. Make the effort to create a few more social exchanges rather than just the transactional connections, and look for wins you can celebrate virtually, today, rather than waiting for the quarterly team get-together!

Shared experiences and cultural rituals

Along with ensuring you have achieved a balanced ratio of communication with each individual (using Losada's model as a guide), another key focus area of successful teams who have great cultures is investing time in both shared experiences and key rituals.

Share the space, no matter how rarely

Our experience at Pragmatic Thinking and that of a range of our clients who have remote staff and high-functioning cultures is that they religiously follow a key strategy: they invest heavily in creating awesome shared experiences when they do get together face to face.

Sure, they may only come together as a team on very rare occasions, but when they do, they maximise the time and opportunity to connect deeply as human beings rather than just discussing job descriptions or delving into strategy. The legacy of these connections carries on and strengthens relationships at a distance. Neuroscience is starting to really understand the power of these important connections.

Systems and neural complexity specialist Dr Fiona Kerr states that we are hard-wired to connect. Our brains are constantly forming new neural pathways through a process known as neurogenesis. When we come together we literally change each other's brains by creating and stimulating neural pathways. One of the ways this happens is through what Dr Kerr calls 'retinal eye-lock': when we look someone in the eye our retinas actually lock on and both parties map very similar neural pathways in their brains. This is the basis for why we experience a greater sense of connection and empathy when we have the chance to truly sit down and connect with someone. This neurological connection increases our ability to collaborate.

One of the strategies that Dr Kerr suggests for increasing a sense of collaboration among a team—something that's a heightened need for teams that work in remote locations—is to provide opportunities for individuals to work together on a creative or challenging situation.

This research provides an alternative to simply getting your team together for purely social interaction. While the dinner and the round of tennis together are fun, one of the greatest ways that you can maximise your time together as a team and elevate collaboration is to provide shared experiences that encourage creative thinking, that tackle the big-picture issues within the team and that ask team members to work together on ideas.

Interestingly, Dr Kerr's research found that, if people's brains were scanned while they are collaborating on something that's highly stimulating, there would be a part of their neural pathways that would be mapped. These maps would match the people with whom they are collaborating. So get people on the same page by maximising the time they have together, have them work collaboratively and the strong connections that will be built will carry over to their interactions when they go back to working in remote locations. It's in this that way that we leverage and extend the value of our time together.

This ability to impact someone else's neural pathways through connection is also evident in our ability to impact heightened emotions and calm the other person down. If there's a sensitive issue or an important discussion that needs to be had, try to have this conversation face to face, either in the same location or via Skype.

If you have remotely located team members, do you take time to make the times you come together special ones? It's so important to move past transactional exchange and get to know and trust each other on a deeper level.

Rituals bind behaviour

Along with investing effort into creating wonderful shared experiences, another area for forming culture and helping to navigate the tough stuff is creating regular rituals that all staff take part in. Being in a different space doesn't mean they can't deeply immerse themselves in the collective spirit of 'what we do around here'. In fact, if you don't make this effort to include remote-located staff into shared rituals, you will undoubtedly create a divide that will lead to many more tough conversations down the track.

Case study: Churchill Education — 'Angels and Mortals'

The move towards a global workforce is a deep challenge for some, yet for others it is a cornerstone to their success. Registered training organisation Churchill Education has built an incredibly successful business, but more importantly, a phenomenal culture, regardless of the remote locations of its employees.

Boasting a team of more than 100 based in three different countries and time zones, this progressive business has invested heavily in shared experiences and carefully considered rituals to bring the team together in spite of the geographical barriers.

(continued)

Case study: Churchill Education — 'Angels and Mortals' *(cont'd)*

One of the rituals all employees at Churchill Education engage in at the end of each year is Angels and Mortals. Every December, in an act of gratitude and creativity, each team member is assigned as a 'silent' Angel for another employee. Often this can be someone in another country, and often they've never even met in person!

The task as an Angel is to bless their Mortal (another employee) a minimum of three times in the month, trying not to let the Angel's halo fall — an objective of the ritual is to try to remain anonymous as the person handing out the blessings.

There have been special meals delivered, hand crafted notes, gifts for children and many inventive ways that Churchill employees have 'blessed' each other in their efforts as Angels. It's certainly fun for everyone involved, but the ritual serves on many layers other than creating happiness.

Not only does Angels and Mortals create a shared experience and yearly ritual, it helps a remote workforce find out more about each other on a deeper level and build deeper bonds of trust. To be a good Angel you have to look into your Mortal's life — find out what they like and don't like. What are their special interests and what do they hold dear to their heart? Arguably the most important outcome of this brilliant cultural ritual is that the participants see each other as human beings and not simply transactional exchanges within the work day.

Conclusion

There's little doubt managing remotely located team members is an advanced challenge worthy of your skills, especially if you're used to having all your team under the same roof. Moreover, addressing the tough conversation with someone via technology is a different beast from tackling it face to face. But it certainly isn't unachievable.

Spend time building a solid culture and making sure you include all team members, not just the ones in the central office. This will reduce conflict and make the pathway much easier when it does occur. You've been blessed to lead teams of talented people from around the country or even the world. Don't squander that talent by not following the principles, ratios and suggestions outlined in this chapter. Your team deserves better, but more importantly, you deserve better.

Darren's insights

Given many workplace leaders tend to ignore or avoid tough conversations at the best of times, dealing with the tough stuff via remote conversations is far too often an easy out. But this is simply the calling card for the underperforming and uncaring manager, not the engaged leader. Throughout my experience coaching, training and consulting to thousands of people, one thing is irrefutable: good managers find a way to deliver outcomes in the tough conversations regardless of the barriers that exist.

Sure, you may have a team that's scattered all over the world, but you also live in a time where the ability to connect regularly has never been easier and as we've discussed throughout this book, you need to build a regular culture of communication for the tough stuff to be conducted well.

Don't make geography an excuse for not doing your job well, especially in an age where technology goes a long way to overcoming the tyranny of distance.

Alison's insights

The idea of leading and managing remote teams can instil fear into many managers—not because they don't believe they can do it, but because it's human nature to focus on the fires in front of us, potentially ignoring what we don't see. The flip side of this is that we make assumptions when we don't have all the information and it's easy to slip into not trusting our staff if we don't hear from them or they don't get back to us immediately (despite the fact they were out at lunch).

If this is the case, recognise your role in bringing fear to the situation. My belief is that rather than start with fear and trepidation, you need to start with trust as your default: trust that the staff you have working remotely want to do a great job and want to give value in their role and trust that you have the skills to manage the process. You also need to trust your intuition when you feel like something needs to be addressed.

In my experience having worked with remote teams, as well as directly managing remote employees, the more you sit on something that you know needs to be addressed, the more it festers. The result is that often you avoid the person you actually need to connect with, leaving them feeling more isolated in an already isolating situation. This is not the recipe for motivation and productivity.

Sean's insights

Rapport, rapport, rapport! My experience of working remotely with clients across the globe for more than a decade now is that we can't emphasise enough the need to put extra time and energy into building the personal human connection with your *remotees*. We talked about it earlier in this chapter, and it can't be said enough: the sense of personal connection is what keeps remote staff going strong through the long periods when you are physically disconnected. If you tend to skirt around the edges of the personal, even when you are face to face with a team member, you are going to be doubly challenged to get stuck into it with remote staff. Perhaps it's time to get a coach, do some human skills training, do whatever you need to do to build your confidence and capability for engaging with people on that authentic human level. Get the human connections right and watch your remote team exceed expectations!

Chapter summary

- If conflict or niggles do occur, act quickly. Don't sit on them and wait for the next time you see each other face to face.

- Check in on your ratio of positive–negative and keep it on the right side of 3:1. Don't default to transaction only.

- Work hard to include remote staff in your cultural rituals.

- Invest deeply in shared experiences when you do come together. You'll rewire each other's brains.

- When conflict is high, use the most personal medium you can to overcome the perception bias that may take place in the gaps.

HUMAN EMOTIONS

are at the

HEART

of all

TOUGH STUFF.

6

DEALING WITH THE GRUFF STUFF
Addressing anger and managing high emotions

If we surveyed 100 people and asked them what the hardest part of dealing with the tough stuff is, 99 responses would be about dealing with emotions. Emotions make things tough, and they are the reason that tough conversations exist. But who would want to live without them? Emotions provide the light and the shade in our lives.

Leaders and managers used to be told to keep a stiff upper lip and not show emotion—to remove emotion from the situation at hand and just deal with the facts. Presenting one face when your body and thoughts scream another is not something you can mask. Despite all your efforts to mask emotions, they will come out in some form and people have an innate ability to pick up on this. They see the inconsistency between what you say and what your body language, tone of voice and behaviours are telling them. Emotions are always at play, so we need to reframe the role that emotions play in the workplace. We need to view emotions as a catalyst for change and the fuel that drives the engine of productivity and innovation. Emotions are awesome!

But emotions also create and drive conflict and heartache. Mapping a pathway through an emotion-laden environment is tough—it's the very heart of the tough stuff. The reality is that you will never separate emotions from your work—never. Individuals who excel at dealing with the tough stuff are those who have learned, and even mastered, the art of managing emotions. So, instead of spending energy and time in trying to push aside, suppress or ignore emotions, it is a far better use of your energy to learn how to manage them well.

Emotions: ignore them at your peril

Managers who fall into the trap of dealing only with facts and figures work hard to remove emotions from the decisions and choices they make. The problem is that working hard to not allow emotions to get in the way is pointless. It is impossible to ignore them because emotions (our own and others') are part of every decision we make and part of every conversation and interaction we have with others, whether you recognise it or not.

Developing an awareness of emotions, and being able to manage and use emotions effectively (a skill described as emotional intelligence), is an important part of successful leadership. According to Daniel Goleman, author of several best-selling books about emotional intelligence, emotional intelligence accounts for 85 to 95 per cent of the difference between mediocre managers and effective, successful leaders.

Consider the best managers you have had throughout your working career. What were the key qualities that stood out about them—the qualities that made them great at their job? We would hazard at a guess that it's not their capacity to balance a budget, or their expertise with spreadsheets or rostering. These are important, but not the skills that great managers are remembered for. Some of the qualities of great managers that come to mind are:

- they are approachable
- they care about others
- they make decisions that are fair.

Often, the qualities that we remember about great and effective managers are associated with their capacity to connect with others, to manage their own and others' emotions, and to make decisions that are fair and that consider the impact on others.

Any time you are dealing with tough stuff, remember that the very reason it is tough is because of human emotions. Your own emotions and the emotions of other people will be involved. There is no way of getting around it; there *will* be emotions and you *will* have to deal with them.

Allow others to own their own emotions

Feeling emotions enriches our lives. They drive passion and purpose within a workplace and can be a great source of joy and fulfilment for employees, and for the organisation's customers and stakeholders. But the reality is that if you get two or more people together for an extended time there will be occasional tension.

Often managers and leaders will delay, dilute or even change the context of a situation to help ease or soften a tough conversation and avoid hurting someone, and so they are not at the receiving end of any strong emotions. They do this in the hope that people will keep a lid on it. The number one thing to remember when dealing with emotions in tough conversations is this: always allow people to own their emotions. Never try to own them for them.

Respect the other person enough to allow them to own and experience whatever emotion arises from the situation. Treat them like an adult; cushioning them from bad or sad news does not do them any favours and does not give them a chance to grow and develop. Any and all emotions they experience are acceptable. The actions that occur as a result of these emotions may be appropriate or inappropriate at work, but the emotions themselves are okay. Emotions are not the enemy; we always have a choice about what we *do* with our emotions. Give others the respect to make this choice themselves.

Anger and actions are two separate things

Within the workplace, anger can be the source of arguments, conflict, aggressive behaviour and even harassment. This is the gruff stuff that most of us will go to great lengths to avoid. But there is a clear distinction between experiencing an emotion and choosing to act a certain way because of it. Emotions are acceptable; the actions that come from them may or may not be. If we go back to the example of Sue and John in the preface, Sue had a wide range of options for responding to her feelings of anger about John's note. Unfortunately, the behaviours she chose grew into longstanding interpersonal unrest within the team. If she had chosen different actions, this scenario may have had a different outcome.

Consider the following actions that people may take after feeling angry about a restructure announcement at work. They may:

- storm into the boss's office for a heated discussion
- go from colleague to colleague to voice their anger and gather support
- write a letter to the CEO demanding an explanation
- start a petition
- bring it up at the next team meeting
- start applying for other jobs
- keep quiet, continue working and keep their anger to themselves (choosing to explode about the dirty dishes in the tea-room instead).

There are countless other options, too, and no doubt you have examples you could add to this list of what people do when they feel angry. When anger is heightened we lose our ability to connect with the rational and logical part of our brain, and this is when irrational and unacceptable behaviour often occurs. Being able to manage this high emotion involves recognising what's happening and taking practical steps to reconnect with our rational thinking.

The cornerstone of being able to address anger and manage high emotions is in understanding what happens in our emotional brain and what we can do to avoid a situation getting to boiling point. Let's explore the emotional centre in our brain.

Tour of the emotional brain

Emotions are experienced in our brain. Understanding where they are experienced, how this part of the brain has developed over time and how it affects other parts of the brain is integral to mastering the ability to manage high emotions. You can see the different parts of the brain in figure 6.1.

Figure 6.1: major parts of the human brain

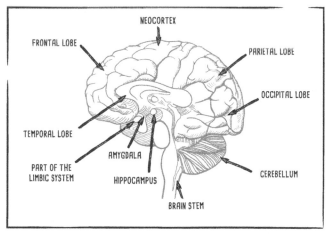

The cerebellum is responsible for most of our motor coordination, including walking. It takes care of the things that we do automatically and don't have to think about very much.

The brain stem controls the body's automatic systems. These are the things we do not need to think about that keep us alive, including our heart beat, blood flow, digestion and breathing.

The neocortex, and in particular the prefrontal area, includes our sense of logic, language and reasoning. This part of the brain is what sets humans apart from the rest of the animal world, and it is truly extraordinary.

In the middle part of the brain is our emotional centre, the limbic system. Our limbic system is often referred to as the 'reptilian brain' because it is underdeveloped compared with the rest of the brain. If we looked at the brain of a reptile, such as a crocodile, we would see no defined neocortex, but they do have a limbic system. Even a crocodile has emotions. Maybe there are crocodile tears after all?

The limbic system has a number of structures, but the one we are most interested in for dealing with the gruff stuff is the amygdala. *Amygdala* is a Latin hybrid word for 'almond'. Our amygdala is an almond-shaped gland within our limbic system that performs a primary role in processing memory and emotional reactions. It is linked to the experience of high emotions, including fear, rage and pleasure.

The amygdala is our ready response team, not just for our brain but for our body, too. It's like a trip wire, and once it's off and running there's no stopping it. The amygdala takes over our emotions, our responses and our behaviours.

Twenty thousand years ago when we were sitting in a cave and a sabre-toothed tiger wandered into the front of the cave, our amygdala kicking into gear was a life-saver. The amygdala gets us into action, fast. The amygdala's response has been measured as being 80000 times faster than our thought processes—our brain and body were responding to the threat before we had even thought, 'There's a sabre-toothed tiger in our cave'. Instead, the amygdala would have the cave-dweller's body upright and running well before any thought process entered the brain. The amygdala takes over our body in what we call an amygdala hijack. When we flip out, it's the amygdala taking over—it shuts down a bunch of pathways, including the pathway to logic and rationality.

In his book *Emotional Intelligence*, Daniel Goleman talks about temperature gradients in the brain. When we are angry or enraged, the temperature in our brain starts to increase, and at a certain point the amygdala actually starts to shut down the prefrontal cortex so that we stop thinking rationally. It stops language and we stop thinking when we hit a rage state. When people say, 'I was so angry I was losing my mind', the reality is they were losing the best part of it. The amygdala hijack is a bit like hypothermia: when you get really cold your body shuts down the blood supply to your legs and slowly conserves it to the areas that need it. When faced with threat, the amygdala heats up, shuts down the things it does not need and helps us get into action.

In the workplace we only occasionally have a sabre-toothed tiger walk into our office. From memory, his name is Bob.

Emotions at work: addressing anger and sadness

The two most common emotions that people try to avoid at work are anger and sadness. When they are heightened, both anger and sadness can be difficult to address and manage. It is these heightened emotions that are worth looking at in order to improve your management skills in the workplace.

When people have emotions that are running high (such as anger, frustration or sadness), they are not (biologically) in a position to make rational decisions. High emotions generally stem from the midbrain region, where the limbic system lies, and subsequent temperature rises within the brain contribute to the disconnection of the logic centres.

What to do when faced with anger

If you are faced with anger or hostility from a staff member, it is important to remember that the anger is not usually directed at you: the anger is often about a process or decision. The other person may be pointing this anger at you, but it has more to do with how the process or decision has affected them. In this situation you need to show respect to the person while still being assertive about the issue (we will look at assertiveness in chapter 7). It is imperative you remain rational so you can direct the conversation well.

The first thing to do is to stay calm. It sounds obvious, but if we can stay calm and steer clear of the increased temperature gradient without losing the plot ourselves, then we're in a better place to access our rational thought process. As soon as our own temperature increases we start to lose control, then the other person loses control too and a completely irrational conversation ensues, one that both of us may regret.

The second point is to keep the tone and the volume of your voice underneath the other person's. Nightclub bouncers who are good at their job understand and use this principle really well. Two things determine whether it is going to be a busy night for a bouncer: the full moon and how loud the guys on the door are. We can't do much about the moon, but we can do a lot about how loud our voice is.

Case study: Dan on the town

Dan is at a bar on a Friday evening and is told by the bar staff that he has had enough to drink. His response is, 'No, I haven't had enough'. His anger and aggression increase and at this point the bar staff contact security.

The bouncer moves through the crowd, walks up to Dan and says, 'Excuse me mate, you've had too much to drink. Time to go,' to which Dan replies, 'No, I haven't. I'm just getting started'. So the bouncer says, raising his voice, 'No, I said you've had enough,' and then the situation starts to escalate.

They start to shout over the top of each other and suddenly Dan's losing all sense of rationality whatsoever. Being inebriated means that he gets to this point, where nothing makes sense, really quickly. He is ready to rumble with a guy big enough to bench press a car.

A bouncer who stays calm would have allowed Dan to stay calm too, keeping the amygdala out of the picture.

Keep it down: the role of tone of voice

Taking steps to keep others connected with the rational part of their brain, even in heightened situations, helps minimise the impact of behaviours acted out in anger. A key step is to re-enter the conversation underneath the tone of the other person. If you imagine having a conversation with someone in which one of you is whispering and the other person is shouting, the shouter is having by far the more uncomfortable experience. Individuals do not usually sustain shouting for very long if the other party doesn't reciprocate the intensity or loudness of voice. So keep your volume down and your voice even and others will start to reciprocate.

Radio silence: cease all conversation

Another technique is to cease conversation. And we mean *all* conversation. We know we can have a conversation without saying a word through our facial expressions, our body language and where we focus our eyes—it's possible to stop talking and still say a lot. Actually, this is often when heated conversations can get to boiling point. So in stopping conversation, you stop all communication—you give nothing back and you're a blank slate.

This approach can be effective quite quickly in cutting into a heated moment. It's like radio silence. When the radio presenter misses a track or an introduction, the silence seems to go on forever, but it's actually only about a second and a half. It has such a major impact that it's like the world has stopped. Radio silence works really well in the moment and provides an ideal position for re-entering the fray using that undertone. Stop all conversation and then come in again quietly. These combinations work well together, and you can use them as often as needed to bring rationality back into the discussion.

Depersonalise and decontaminate

In chapter 4 we discussed how to use non-verbal communication, in particular where to direct the attention in the conversation in order to depersonalise and decontaminate conversation effectively. These strategies, including the use of three-point communication, are particularly effective in avoiding escalation of anger in heated conversations.

Safety is paramount

While there are steps and measures you can take to maintain rationality in heated conversations, there are times and situations when rational behaviour has been superseded by irrational behaviour. The reality is that conversations born out of anger may turn aggressive, and your personal safety is paramount. If someone is extremely volatile, seek support and backup from others and defer conversation until there's a time and place where a more rational conversation can be had.

Tips for dealing with anger

There are many tips and techniques you can use to deal with anger in the workplace.

- Stay calm while still being firm.

- Always keep the volume of your voice underneath the other person's and do not allow the situation to escalate.

- Allow the person the opportunity to calm down by ceasing communication for a short time and then returning to it once they (and you) have calmed down, using undertone again.

- Recognise that things said in anger are not usually grounded in fact or reason. Anger utilises an ancient part of the brain and does not fully engage our higher centres of thinking. Anger does not make hurtful things acceptable, but it usually isn't a true indication of how someone feels.

- If someone is extremely volatile, safety is paramount. This is not the time to try to have a rational discussion. Cease the conversation if you feel unsafe by deferring to another time when you are more likely to be able to achieve a resolution. If necessary, involve a third party.

What to do when faced with sadness

Many managers feel awkward about dealing with tears and sadness at work. Often the discomfort that comes when someone starts crying in front of you is your own discomfort. Your instinct may be to do whatever you can to stop them crying, although this is often more about you wanting to feel comfortable again rather than wanting to support the other person. What matters is that you validate their experience and acknowledge their sadness.

When it comes to addressing sadness and tears at work, it is imperative to understand the distinction between sympathy and empathy. These are discussed further in chapter 7, but are worth a brief mention here. Sympathy may be words such as, 'I feel bad for you', and 'I'm sorry that's happening to you'. The unspoken message that sympathy ultimately portrays is, 'I'm glad it's you and not me'. On the other hand, empathy comes from a place of being able to connect with the emotions that others are experiencing: 'It looks like you're really struggling with this', and 'It sounds like it must be tough for you'. When we express empathy we validate someone's experience.

Tears are not a sign of weakness; they are a sign of humanness. We have witnessed great leaders display their passion, vulnerability and compassion through tears, and often our response is actually to feel a greater connection with them. Witnessing raw emotions can connect us together in a way that words alone would not. Researcher and expert on shame and vulnerability Brené Brown suggests that our capacity to be vulnerable is the key to becoming a leader with influence. As a manager, leader and colleague it is important that you recognise that tears and sadness are okay. Don't be afraid to allow others the space to show this and don't be afraid to unveil your own humanness if the situation arises.

Tips for dealing with tears

The following tips may help you when you're confronted with tears in the workplace.

- Allow the other person to cry; don't feel that you have to stop them.

- Offering tissues is a simple empathic gesture that gives you both something to do and says, 'It's okay to cry'.

- Simple statements such as 'It's okay' are fine in this situation.

- Your silence can also be okay, as this allows the other person to compose themselves again.

- You can acknowledge the validity of the other person's behaviour by expressing empathy. You might say, 'This is upsetting for you', or 'It sounds like this has had a considerable impact upon you'.

Conclusion

Robert Townsend, former CEO of Avis, has said, 'A good manager doesn't try to eliminate conflict; he tries to keep it from wasting the energies of his people. If you're the boss and your people fight you openly when they think that you are wrong—that's healthy'.

You will need to deal with gruff stuff at work from time to time. It's inevitable that people get angry or sad, or experience any one of the hundreds of emotions that could arise in a day. The first stage of getting better at dealing with heightened emotion is acceptance, not ignorance. By accepting that emotions will have to be dealt with, you can make sure you are better equipped to predict, manage and deal with these situations and achieve an outcome that respects everyone involved.

Darren's insights

Show me a workplace team that can effectively deal with heightened emotions in a public, constructive fashion, and I will show you a team of high performers.

The hallmarks of innovative, agile teams and businesses are behaviours in which they challenge each other's beliefs and the collective status quo to achieve great things. That doesn't come without some pain. Having your behaviour challenged or questioned can hurt, but excellence in any form requires effort and a little pain.

Workplaces have to trust each other more, and trust that if I say something that hurts or upsets someone or makes them angry, then the roof won't cave in. Too many organisations and teams tiptoe around each other's emotions: if you look deeper, this behaviour says, 'I don't trust you', or 'I don't trust me'. Neither is a good way to build excellence.

Alison's insights

Addressing anger and managing high emotions should not be avoided, so it is crucial that you are equipped to understand how to deal with these emotions—both your own and others'. Anger often comes from a place of feeling hurt, invalidated or undervalued—where people feel like they have not been listened to or their point of view has not been considered or heard. Exceptional leaders and managers can not only listen to what is being said in the heat of the moment, but also hear what is not being said.

Think about the last time you were faced with someone expressing anger or frustration. What was the person upset about? Why might they have been feeling hurt, invalidated, undervalued or disconnected? In your own language, find ways of expressing your understanding and compassion. From here you can move towards finding a solution to the situation together.

Sean's insights

Every time I get into a discussion about emotions, I cannot help jumping into a tirade about judgement. We have learned to judge our emotions, particularly the gruff ones, rather than accept them for what they are. At work and at home, we make ourselves, and others, feel it's wrong to even experience them in the first place.

A first step in being powerful in the face of heated emotional responses is to see them as a normal, human thing—nothing to be judged, just something to be accepted and acted upon in functional ways. Emotions are there for a reason—let's understand those reasons as quickly as possible, before the emotions escalate. When you don't listen and respond to your own emotion, it just gets louder. When you don't allow a staff member's emotion to be heard, it also gets louder. Judge behaviours, not feelings, and you will go a long way in managing the gruff stuff.

Chapter summary

- Exceptional managers are skilled at dealing with emotions.

- Always allow others to own their own emotions; don't own them for them.

- Feeling angry and acting out of anger are two separate things.

- In an amygdala hijack we lose access to our rational thinking, so work hard at not having the amygdala come into the game.

- When dealing with anger from others, keep your tone of voice down, cease communication for a short time and depersonalise the conversation.

- When dealing with tears, allow the other person to cry, offer empathic statements and remember that tears are not a sign of weakness—they are a sign of humanness.

- Avoid becoming an emotionless leader. Here's a truth: you can't be emotionless anyway!

Resistance to
CHANGE
is predictable,
but with the right tools,
FEAR CAN BE
TRANSFORMED INTO
CONFIDENCE.

7

DEALING WITH THE HUFF STUFF

Dealing with resistant, defensive and stubborn behaviour

Have you noticed that the world is changing? And it's changing quickly! Never before have we had to be more adaptable, flexible and fast moving to keep up with change than we do right now. Your organisation has almost certainly faced some degree of change in the past six months. It may even be in a constant state of change. Fear not, though: this is now the norm, not the exception.

The notion of a five-year strategic plan has disappeared in this rapidly changing world, and most organisations have realised such a process is guessing, at best—because even with the best resources it's impossible to predict what is required in a fast-changing future. Right now we can't say what the business world might be like in 12 months' time, let alone in five years. Flexible and forward-thinking organisations that not only deal with but also embrace constant change will rise to the top.

But doing that is not as simple as it sounds.

Human beings have an innate resistance to change. Our physiological systems are actually wired to keep us in a state of status quo known as homeostasis. The body constantly regulates its systems to maintain them within certain levels, like our body temperature, our weight, blood glucose levels, metabolism and hormone balances. Genetically, we're programmed to resist major changes to these internal systems and work hard to maintain equilibrium.

The other innate barrier to change is our internal drive to defend—in this case, defending what we know and the way things are. Uncertainty is one of the biggest threats possible to the survival instincts in the brain because the brain just doesn't know what to do in the space of the unknown. Human beings will go to great lengths to resist change and maintain the status quo, even if we're not entirely happy with the current situation, purely because we know what to expect if we don't change. The unknown is scary.

As a manager and leader in this rapidly changing world, and rapidly changing work environment, it's likely you have already faced resistance, defensiveness and stubborn behaviour at work. This chapter provides practical tips on how to achieve results from the key conversations needed to move people beyond resistant, defensive and stubborn behaviour and step forward into growth. The cornerstone of this approach is using effective assertiveness, but first let's explore the huff stuff in some detail.

Resistant behaviour

One of the keys to influencing change in others is being able to work with their resistance to it.

Resistant behaviour comes in many shapes and forms. It may be someone generally dragging their heels—showing a lack of action or motivation to do what needs to be done. Often resistant behaviour is expressed during periods of change, such as change of work flow or work roles, change in team dynamics, and even change experienced as a result of the big three—restructures, redundancies and dismissals (which are discussed in chapter 9).

Resistance can also crop up in people's language: 'Yes, that sounds good, but ...', or 'I'm just playing devil's advocate here ...'. Statements such as these can be indicators that someone is not really onboard and is either seeking more information or seeking to railroad the process.

When we're faced with resistant behaviour it's often our natural tendency to defend the change; that is, to try to convince someone of all the reasons they shouldn't feel the way they do.

While your argument or decision may be valid, all this conversation does is strengthen the other person's resistance because they haven't felt heard or understood. Have you ever experienced this—trying to convince someone to see your point of view only to have them dig in their heels even further?

Case study: Shannon and Billie

At their weekly team meeting, Shannon, the team manager, discusses the importance of team members sharing their work tasks and case loads with others in the team so that the team can be more efficient in covering queries from customers, particularly when staff are on leave or away from the office. She asks the team members to sit down together over the coming week to go over their case loads and progress.

(continued)

Case study: Shannon and Billie *(cont'd)*

Billie is resistant to briefing the team on the status of her cases and says that she feels this is a waste of valuable time, particularly because they are so busy at the moment. Shannon starts to defend the decision in an attempt to convince Billie of her point of view by telling Billie all the reasons why collaborating is essential to team effectiveness.

Billie defends her position even more strongly and the conversation quickly gets into a heated discussion with both parties continuing to state their point of view, so they end up going around in circles.

After the team meeting, Shannon realises that defending her position in the conversation did not prove effective and decides to approach Billie again, this time in a calm manner and with a willingness to understand Billie's perspective and concerns rather than simply defending her own position.

As a result, Billie is able to express to Shannon how stressed she is over a particularly difficult case, and that she is already working long hours and feels that an additional meeting is another thing added to her already long to-do list. As a result of this discussion and becoming clearer about Billie's resistance, they are able to work together on how to deal with the tough case at hand and how to reduce Billie's case load overall for the time being until the case is finalised. It is at this point that Billie says she could see that other people in the team understanding her workload would be helpful and agrees to make the time to sit down with other team members that week.

Rather than defend your position straight away, rolling with resistance and uncovering what underlies it can help to overcome resistant behaviour at work.

Reasons for resistance

There can be a whole range of reasons why someone is resistant, over and above our innate tendency to resist change. It may be that similar strategies have been attempted in the past and were unsuccessful, which has led to scepticism. It may be that change is threatening to their job role.

Resistance commonly arises when there's a change, or even a perceived change, to people's work. Most people are instinctively concerned about any strategy that could see their role changing, their workload increasing, their job or part of it being given to someone else or even being given more responsibility than they have now, like Billie's resistance in the case study.

Many individuals have a strong work identity: who they are as a person is closely linked to what they do for a job. You've been there when meeting someone new: 'So, what do you do?' is generally the first question after an introduction. The work we do is inherently connected with how others see us and how we see ourselves. So, if there's a change to someone's job title, workload or responsibilities, resistance is highly likely.

Resistance may also come from a lack of job security, or the perception of it. Nothing sparks up our drive to defend more than the notion that our job and financial situation are not as secure as we thought they were.

More than six decades ago, psychologist and founder of the *Journal of Humanistic Psychology* Abraham Maslow contended there are levels of human needs that form a pecking order, requiring us to satisfy one need before moving on to the next (see figure 7.1, overleaf).

Figure 7.1: Maslow's hierarchy of needs

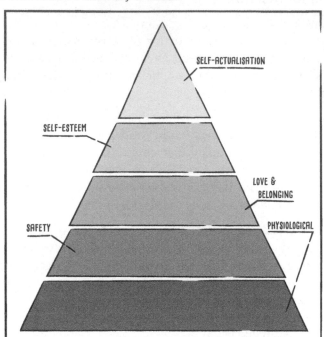

If we consider Maslow's hierarchy of needs, our ability to provide and supply food and shelter for ourselves and our family is our number-one need. If something at work looks like it may threaten this need, human nature dictates our resistance to it. The ability for us to view things rationally or think of things beyond our circumstance is nigh on impossible.

Moving up the hierarchy, human beings also have an innate drive to bond and feel a sense of belonging to a group. This can be attained in the workplace through friendships and being a valued member of the team. If changes at work look like they could change the group dynamics, affect key relationships, or limit or inhibit the ability to bond with others, it's natural that individuals will resist this.

Maslow's next level covers esteem, achievement and the need to feel a sense of competency and mastery over a task or project. For some people, these aspects of the job are highly important. If this need is threatened, individuals will respond with resistance.

Understanding that there can be a variety of reasons for resistant behaviour allows you as a manager and leader to grasp the wider context behind the behaviours you see in the workplace. Such understanding isn't about making these behaviours acceptable, but if you understand them, you will be better placed to do something about them.

Dealing with resistance

The first strategy in dealing with resistant behaviour is to roll with the resistance. Rolling with the resistance means not matching it by reciting every reason for why someone showing resistance shouldn't feel the way they do—your recitation just becomes a sales pitch to someone who is not ready to buy. The risk of pushing too much at this point is that the resister will dig their heels in even more—especially if they believe their standpoint is well founded. Managing resistance is difficult to do well because it can mean giving up your right to be right, even when you *are* right, in order to create outcomes that work better, and to prioritise functionality over ego. If we reflect on Shannon and Billie in the case study, Shannon's decision was well founded and well intentioned, but it wasn't until she gave up the need to defend her position as being the right one that she could have a conversation about what may be getting in the way for Billie. By letting go of her ego she could have a conversation about what the real issue and barrier was. From there it was easier to address the problem and move forward.

The goal is to move someone from being resistant to being receptive to change. In order to do this, people need the opportunity to vent and to have their point of view heard and acknowledged. It's important to realise that you can understand someone's point of view and not agree with it at the same time. This is a particularly powerful skill for a manager to develop. Later in this chapter we will explore the power of empathy, which is the cornerstone for ensuring the other party feels heard.

Amplify ambivalence

One of the traps of resistant behaviour is the person sitting on the fence. This person has yet to make a clear decision and is stuck as to the direction they will take. This is an unnerving place to be for too long. An effective manager has the ability to influence and support others to get off the fence and make a decision. Managers can do this by highlighting or amplifying the ambivalence and doubt that the indecisive person is experiencing. An effective way to do this is by highlighting a disconnect between what someone says and their actions. For example, 'So, I hear you want to work with this team, but I also get the sense there's something holding you back from diving in, boots and all. What's going on?'

Or 'You've expressed your desire to get this project up and running for a while now, but to date nothing's happened. Is there anything getting in the way?'

These are key conversations that managers must have with staff battling uncertainty. They will highlight the ambivalence and help sort through what's getting in the way to move the person towards actually making a decision.

Dance, don't drag

Dealing with resistance can be like dancing the waltz with a shy partner. Part of the art of dancing is leading, but when there's resistance, it's far more effective (and graceful) to move with your partner when they back off, rather than dragging them along. When the resistance subsides, you can lead again.

Be confident and assured when you lead at work, but remember that heavy-handedness will result in two things:

- Creating an unwilling partner.
- Doing all the hard work yourself.

No dance is fun in that environment.

Defensive behaviour

We have already mentioned that a key driver in human behaviour is the drive to defend. Animals get defensive the moment they feel they have no options or that their options are being severely limited. At work it's the metaphorical equivalent to being backed into a corner and there being no way out. Human beings operate much the same way as any other animal—we just don't snarl and bare our teeth (usually).

Often what sits at the very core of defensive behaviour is fear: it may be fear of the unknown, fear of an uncertain future or fear of having no options.

Be aware that there may be some strong external factors contributing to someone feeling defensive at work. The person may be the family's breadwinner, and be relying on the job to feed mouths and clothe backs.

If defensiveness is protection against threat or attack, we need to reduce the fear component that accompanies a threat or attack—whether it is real or perceived—in order to deal with defensiveness effectively.

Turn fear into confidence

According to Marcus Buckingham, *The New York Times* best-selling author of *One Thing You Need to Know*, one of the three principles of leadership is the ability to turn fear into confidence. Resistance and defensive, stubborn behaviour are often borne from a sense of fear and trepidation.

Nothing is more contagious than the confidence of others, especially the confidence of our leaders. For confidence to be respected it needs to be genuine and trustworthy—more than just an optimistic Pollyanna viewpoint. Leaders who speak and act with confidence, particularly in the face of change and uncertainty, command great influence and loyalty. So how do we turn fear into confidence? Try the following three tips.

Clear the road

One of the ways to turn fear into confidence is to talk about a joint vision of the future that is clear and compelling. Too often, as leaders, we have a pathway mapped out but fail to explain it to others. Fear is an easily generated emotion when coupled with uncertainty. To help others to get more certainty and to focus on the same picture you are seeing, you need to provide more detailed context. Engage them in a discussion on the why, what and how of your big picture. And then go a step further. To put a rocket on confidence around vision, go beyond the audible forms of communication, and move into visual communication. Map out a process flowchart or draw a model. It helps people anchor where they are and where they need to be.

Start with gratitude

Gratitude has often been described as the healthiest of all emotions. It makes sense that if you want to maintain a healthy, trustful relationship you use the power of gratitude. Instead of simply expecting someone to be physically present for a role or task, try thanking them for being onboard, for their skills or even for their cautiousness in moving forward. Gratitude communicates your confidence in others. It's a sure-fire way to make people feel more confident in themselves!

Reinforce the good stuff

If someone feels like they are standing on the end of the 10-metre diving platform, and you push them over the proverbial edge with embarrassing or critical tactics, they are not going to be too quick to put themselves in the same position again. They will resist tooth and nail.

Sometimes taking on a new task at work can feel like standing on the end of that platform. Filling people up with encouragement and praise so they choose to make the leap themselves (rather than shoving them off in a defensive state of anxiety) will go a long way to building confidence in the long run. Look for quick wins and reward them accordingly.

Stubborn behaviour

Certain personality traits are desirable for certain jobs. Someone pedantic with an acute attention to detail, who's a perfectionist in everything they do, is the kind of person you want doing your tax return, flying your plane or performing surgery on a loved one. But this type of personality trait may be dysfunctional for someone in a work environment that is filled with constant change, innovation, creativity or problem solving. Getting bogged down in the detail will see them fall behind the pack.

As far as personality traits go, stubbornness can be highly regarded in some settings, but in others it can be detrimental to teamwork.

When looking at stubborn behaviour, it is worth considering that stubbornness is negatively correlated with expressiveness. In other words, when people are acting stubbornly, they may not know how to express what they feel through language, so they refuse to budge. Because their ability to put their thoughts into words is underdeveloped (in a particular situation) they will shut down and communicate less.

So when confronted by stubborn behaviour, consider the following points.

It's not all about you

Don't take stubbornness personally—it isn't about you. It's as simple as that. Sometimes when faced with stubborn behaviour we can start our own internal dialogue, much of which can be egocentric. The problem is that, by personalising stubbornness you add another layer to a situation that doesn't need it. Stubbornness is a trait and it probably developed long before you ever walked into their lives. Repeat again, 'It's not about me'.

Assess alignment

Check to see whether you are both on the same page. Stubbornness is often related to dialogue (both internal and external), so check that you are both clear on the topic or strategy. Possibly, you have been using two-point communication (as we discussed in chapter 4), which uses speech as the primary communication medium. The problem with this is that as little as 20 per cent of people process their learning through auditory channels. Our suggestion? Use a visual medium (three-point communication) that you both look at in order to process the information. A whiteboard is our favourite, but a piece of paper works nearly as well. Often stubbornness can be overcome simply by clearing up the main points you want to achieve or by better understanding the other person's point of view.

In the case study, Shannon and Billie's heated discussion during the team meeting was conducted with two-point communication, leaving both parties feeling like they needed to defend their personal points of view. The discussion between Shannon and Billie after the meeting would have been very effective using three-point communication, writing out the key issues on a piece of paper and having both Shannon and Billie refer to this object. It is much easier to get on the same page using this process (pun intended!).

Watch yourself

When faced with stubbornness, getting upset or angry will not make the situation any better—it will only make it worse. So beware of your own physical and emotional responses in the face of someone else's stubborn behaviour, and ensure you remain calm, polite and friendly. Don't underestimate the power of modelling the behaviours you want to see in others.

* * *

Having explored defensive, resistant and stubborn behaviour, we will now look at the overarching method for dealing with any huff stuff. Assertiveness is the critical process to employ for achieving success in this area.

Assertiveness and empathy

Assertiveness is about putting your needs and opinions forward, but it is not about doing this at any cost—that strategy is more like communication by intimidation.

Assertive communication involves seeking a win–win for both parties, taking into account the needs of others. It's as important for one person to put their thoughts, ideas and needs forward as it is to consider the other person's point of view.

Traditional assertiveness approaches have focused too much on the concept of ownership, particularly in our language. Using 'I', 'me' or 'my' statements to own the process, while well intentioned, can also succeed in turning a mild-mannered person into a mini-dictator.

While we promote the importance of presenting your own needs, you also need to consider the vitally important role of empathy in being assertive. Empathy is the counterpoint to presenting your own needs, and the use of both these elements provides the formula for true assertiveness.

Therefore, our definition of assertiveness is:

assertiveness = empathy + presenting your own needs.

In the words of Stephen Covey, the author of *The 7 Habits of Highly Effective People*, 'Seek first to understand and then to be understood'.

Empathy: seek first to understand

Have you ever felt completely understood by someone else, believing that they totally 'got' what you were feeling and thinking?

That's empathy: a capacity to recognise or understand another's state of mind or emotion. It's often described as the ability to put yourself in another person's shoes.

Complete understanding of another person's point of view is impossible. But if you're empathic, you can get a clearer understanding of what's going on for the other person.

The confusion between sympathy and empathy

Too often sympathy is confused with empathy. There is little confusion of either of these terms with apathy, which is a lack of interest or concern. Both sympathy and empathy are states of concern, but the origins of that concern distinguish them from each other.

Sympathy is the feeling of compassion for someone else: the wish to see them better off or happier. It is often described as 'feeling sorry for' someone. It's worth considering that underneath sympathy is often a sense of 'I'm glad it's not me,' or 'I've been there before', which are both person-centric statements. Make no mistake, sympathy is a wonderful human quality, but in essence, sympathy is actually about you rather than the other person.

Empathy involves a deeper level of understanding that requires sharing another person's emotional state, if only briefly. It's the sense of seeing things as though you're in their shoes. Being empathic means being able to emotionally read other people and then communicate this level of understanding effectively.

Is empathy just giving in? Is being empathic being soft? If I am empathic, won't people just walk over me?

If any of these questions resonate with you, you should reassess your view of the word.

Empathy is not about being mushy or touchy-feely. It's about connecting with and understanding another person's point of view. Empathy isn't a soft skill: it's one of the hardest skills. Consider the following points to help restructure the importance you place on having empathy in your workplace:

- Empathic people are superb at recognising and meeting the needs of others, be they customers, workmates, staff or bosses. (This is the essence of exceptional customer service.)

- Leaders need to understand a talented person's needs, aspirations and motivation in order to keep them. (Business success is based on retaining talent.)

- In a cross-cultural environment, there are always misunderstandings or communication difficulties. These can primarily be overcome by using empathy and, in particular, recognition of body-language cues. (In a global world your ability to work cross-culturally is an essential skill.)

The difference between apathy, sympathy and empathy is summed up in these three statements:

- Apathy is 'I don't care how you feel'.

- Sympathy is 'You poor thing'.

- Empathy is 'Looks like you're feeling really down today'.

The style of empathy

The overall style of empathy involves being:

- *authentic*. People have a strong innate ability to pick up false interest a mile away. If you're not authentic when you engage with others, they will know. Be genuinely interested in the other person. This also requires you to be open and transparent about why you're interested in their point of view.

- *inquisitive*. It's easier to reach a deeper level of empathy with someone if you know more about their situation.

- *overt*. We can have a lot of empathic stuff going on in our heads when we listen to someone, but we sometimes forget to say out loud what we see, feel and hear about their current state. If you don't put the empathy out there overtly, and express it explicitly, the other person won't experience your empathy, and the positive impact will be lost.

Empathy in our language

Now that we've made the case for empathy, let's look at how to use its power in your language. Unfortunately, even when we do remember to voice empathy, a disconnect can occur between our perception and our language. In other words, we can sense another's reactions and emotions well, but do a poor job of communicating it.

Much of this disconnect can be attributed to Western society's cultural fixation on person-centric success: in most Western cultures we tend to focus on individual success first and on society second.

It is driven throughout our education systems, our sports and leisure activities and even our language. Some Indigenous Australian and Asian cultures are the reverse: they are society-centric and their members have little to no problem being empathic.

If we were to survey a group of people raised in Western cultures and ask them to give us an empathic statement, overwhelmingly the responses would be prefixed by either one of the following phrases: 'I can see', or 'I can understand'.

Have you noticed the disconnect? Even in our attempts to be empathic, our very first response is to talk about ourselves — 'I can understand'! Clinical academic Professor Tim Usherwood discusses the difference between primary and secondary empathic statements in his work, and following are some examples of the language that is commonly used.

Primary empathic language

Let's look at some language that truly is empathic — what we refer to as primary empathic language.

Some examples of empathic questions are:

- What impact has this had on you?
- How do you feel about what is going on?
- How do you feel about your decision?
- How does this affect you?
- What is your position on what is happening?
- Is there anything else it would be useful for me to know?

Some examples of empathic statements are:

- You look upset...
- It looks like you...
- It sounds like you...
- You look confused.
- You look frustrated.
- You must have been frustrated when you couldn't complete that project because...
- It sounds like this has been a tough time...
- You've been through a lot lately.
- That must have been hard for you to do.
- You don't seem comfortable with that plan.

The common denominator of primary empathic language is the removal of 'I' and not focusing on yourself in the question. Effectively, this serves to talk about the person or process, not about you.

Secondary empathic language

Secondary empathic statements are used when we have entered ourselves into the conversation. These secondary empathic skills work well *after* a primary empathic exchange has taken place.

Assessment statements include:

- I can see that it is very hard for you to talk about this.
- I can appreciate that that must have been frustrating for you.

Checking statements include:

- Correct me if I am wrong...
- Have I got this right...?

Using empathic language and having a greater understanding of the concept of empathy will improve your ability to demonstrate or give voice to empathy.

The other half of the assertiveness equation

Your needs are the other half of the assertiveness equation. This is the area that most assertive coaching focuses on: owning your needs.

Sometimes, in an attempt to be assertive, people barely hint at their own needs, not wanting to be pushy or demanding, but as a result struggle to get their point across. Being assertive, however, is not about being nice, nor is it about being nasty. It's about being effective and clear. In other words, it's about setting clear boundaries in order to give yourself the best chance to achieve a win–win situation for both parties.

Tips for presenting your needs

When presenting your needs for moving forward in a discussion with someone in a huff-stuff conversation, it is important to do the following:

- Assert your needs and wants.
- Clarify the level of intensity.

Assert your needs and wants

Communication breakdowns occur when messages have been misinterpreted or not fully understood by all parties. You need to assert your needs, wants or opinions clearly, and to do that, you must be clear about what your personal needs actually are.

Part of asserting your needs is owning your reactions. It's important to use phrases such as 'I feel...', 'I think...' and 'My take on this is...', rather than talk in general or vague terms. People who struggle to assert their needs will often use phrases such as, 'The boss needs this by tomorrow', or 'Legislation says we have to get this done'. By doing this, they effectively divorce themselves from the need, and yet there is rarely anything more compelling than someone standing in front of you telling you they need something. Own the need and see the results.

Clarify the level of intensity

Each tough-stuff conversation has its own level of importance attached to it. We call this the *level of intensity*. The intensity of the conversation can be driven by a number of factors, such as pressure from deadlines, inertia from one party or impatience from another. Professor of psychology at the University of Washington, Marsha Linehan provides a useful distinction between the level of intensity based on whether you are asking for or refusing something. The key thing to remember is not all conversations require the same level of assertion; you can have greater impact in your conversations by matching the level of intensity to the situation.

For example, Linehan talks about intensity levels if you are asking for something. Low intensity begins with indirectly hinting and then openly hinting; high intensity begins with being firm but still taking 'no', to firm and not taking 'no'.

There is a similar hierarchy of intensity for refusing something. Low level intensity moves from where we express hesitation by saying yes to expressing unwillingness. High level intensity moves from firm refusal but still considering doing it up to firm refusal and not giving in.

You will notice that high intensity levels are very direct in their approach. There isn't very much intention of changing our request or refusal. The low intensity levels are much more collaborative and flexible. The difference between high and low intensity levels is quite distinct and provides the cornerstone towards an effective, assertive approach. Before you step into the conversation, get clear on which intensity level is required in the circumstances.

Now that we've explored both components of assertiveness — empathy and your own needs — let's look at how we can use them together, regardless of the situation.

Solving the assertiveness puzzle

What we know is that empathy is a focus on 'you' (as in the other person). Your own need is a focus on 'I' (me), and so one area in a conversation that we should not forget is a focus on 'we'. These three components give us our process — every exchange in a huff-stuff conversation should contain 'you', 'I' and 'we' in some order.

The intensity of the situation determines the order in which the information is conveyed.

Low intensity levels

Let's say there isn't too much heat in the conversation — it certainly hasn't moved beyond negotiation. Perhaps it is a mid-year performance discussion, or negotiating the roles within a project. If this were the case it would be likely you would apply a low intensity level. The structure for this type of conversation should be:

empathy statement → own needs statement → resolution statement.

In other words, you should move from the 'you' focus to the 'I' focus and finally to a focus on 'we'.

Here are some examples of statements at this intensity level:

- 'This project is important to you [empathy], but having my say is very important to me also [own needs]. We need to reach some common ground or we will be going nowhere fast. If we can work together on this I think we will present a quality product [resolution]'.

- 'You're quite upset by this poor customer feedback review [empathy]. I'm not very happy about this either, as your shift supervisor [own needs], but I think we can work out some better strategies to help us improve in the future [resolution].

High intensity levels

Now let's look at some conversations where the intensity level is much higher. The time for lengthy collaboration or discussion has passed. Perhaps the conversation is with someone who has repeatedly ignored previous requests, or is about an occupational health and safety procedure that has been ignored. In this case a high intensity level might be applied.

The structure for this type of conversation should be:

own needs statement → empathy statement → resolution statement.

In other words, you should move from the 'I' focus to the 'you' focus and finally to the 'we' focus.

Here are some examples of statements at this intensity level:

- 'The way I was spoken to in today's team meeting upset me and made me feel undermined. I don't want that to happen again [own needs]. It sounds like you think my direction in the ABC project is not the same as the way you would handle things [empathy] but we need to present a concerted front to the directors or the funding for our section might be cut [resolution]'.

- 'It's important to me to have a chance to contribute my ideas to the project [own needs]. The project is obviously also very important to you [empathy]. Unless we are able to integrate some of my ideas we may not present the best product [resolution]'.

While we present this theory in sentences, in your practical application it will be time spent, rather than sentences, that reflects intensity. For example, you have 10 minutes to address a topic with a staff member, so you might spend three minutes focusing on empathy (you), two minutes focusing on your own needs (I) and finish the conversation on resolving the discussion together (we).

Finding balance

Using the assertiveness methodology outlined here will help you achieve the balance needed for a tough-stuff conversation. Regardless of how big the conversation is, you will always be able to use empathy, and regardless of how sensitive a situation is, you will always be able to state your own needs. Choose the level of intensity required and apply the relevant conversation structure.

By ensuring both of these elements are included, along with a 'we' closing statement or resolution, you will be a long way towards achieving success in the huff stuff.

Conclusion

In 1933, in his inaugural presidential address, with his country going headlong into the greatest economic depression the world has known, Franklin Delano Roosevelt famously stated, 'The only thing we have to fear is fear itself'. While such a statement may be inspiring, it is also rather challenging, if not impossible, to hear at a time when you're the one trapped by fear. The good news is that defensive, resistant and stubborn behaviour, all borne of fear, can be transformed. With effort, and the right application of some sound behavioural tools, you can shift fear into courage and break through resistance to change.

Darren's insights

Resistance to positions of authority can often be learnt behaviour because of past experience or, in some cases, cultural context. In Australia, for example, there is an anti-authoritarian culture: a leader is seen as someone who has to prove themselves to the lower ranks, rather than the other way around.

So first things first: drop the ego and stop thinking their behaviour is aimed at you personally. It's not. It's about them, their experience or their culture.

Second, when dealing with the huff stuff, examine your own behaviour before you judge someone else's as being defensive. Are you modelling or even leading the behaviour?

Alison's insights

The huff-stuff behaviours are often interpreted as someone being unmotivated, and so there can be a belief that all we need to do is get people motivated. Hence the team-building days that try to get a team excited about a change but end up with team members digging their heels in even further, proving more destructive than constructive.

The reality is that there is no such thing as no motivation. The key to managing resistance and stubbornness is being able to find out what motivates people. If someone resists a project, a task or a new direction, or if you have asked them three times to contact customers and they still haven't done it, then you need to find out what is motivating this resistance—what is driving this behaviour? Finding out people's motivations is far more constructive for moving forward.

Sean's insights

As perennial as change is, so too is human resistance to change. The best thing we can do about this conundrum is practise acceptance for both sides. Non-judgemental acceptance, simply for what is and for the way we are, will create some of the calm necessary to respond to tough and huff stuff. If you struggle with accepting others' resistance to change, my advice is to go ahead and demand extraordinary responsiveness to change and set the standard at platinum, but acknowledge that sometimes you will have to slow down to speed up. Give your people a bit more of your compassion and let them know it is normal to feel the way they do—there is no faster way to get them on your side.

Chapter summary

- It's not all about you—it's about them.

- Roll with resistance. Remember: it's a dance, like the waltz. Sometimes you lead and sometimes you follow.

- Amplify any ambivalence expressed by others to move them out of feeling stuck in making a decision.

- Your most seamless successes will occur when you move people from fear to confidence. Share your vision, speak confidence into their worlds and focus on their good stuff.

- Resist the urge to use force to move someone who is resistant. Use the power of empathy in action to engage them: their needs plus your needs.

- Seek first to understand and then be understood. Use empathy effectively as a key component of all assertive communication.

- Assess the situation and its intensity. If it is high, use the I, you, we order. If intensity is low, use the you, I, we order.

UNCERTAINTY
can create
CHAOS;
**IN TIMES OF RAPID
CHANGE,**
focus on being
EFFECTIVE,
rather than
PERFECT.

8

DEALING WITH THE RAPID STUFF

Addressing the tough issues in a rapid-change environment

Before we get into this chapter, we'd like to ask you a few questions:

- Do you believe the world is getting slower or faster?
- Is it getting simpler or more complex?
- Is it less demanding or more demanding?

Have we cheered you up yet? No doubt, your responses—like those of the thousands of people we've asked these questions—are the same: the world is getting faster, more complex and more demanding. Furthermore, if we'd asked you these same questions five years ago, or even 10 years ago, there's every chance that your responses would have been the same.

Change is not new in our workplaces. It's always been part of how we work, lead and manage. What is different in our workplaces is the sheer speed of change. It's rapid. How you, as a manager, leader and team deal with this rapid stuff—and the conflict that arises with it—will make all the difference in a competitive environment. Your ability to deal with things quickly and to move on—to not hold grudges or waste valuable time on unnecessary conversations—will see you and your team rise to the top. With growing competition in the marketplace, not only for customers but also for talented employees, it's never been a more important time to build a robust feedback culture, one in which tough conversations are addressed effectively.

In addition to an increasingly competitive landscape, we are smack-bang in the middle of the content era. Anything you want answers to can be found online in a matter of milliseconds. Knowing stuff is no longer the advantage it once was—in many cases the sheer accessibility of knowledge is becoming debilitating. It's a noisy world and no doubt you have at times experienced a sense of overwhelm and overload because of the sheer amount of information you need to comprehend, consolidate and deal with on any given day. So it's not hard to understand that if you're feeling overwhelmed then so too are the staff you're leading.

In this chapter we're going to explore some of the psychological changes that are occurring in workplaces as a result of the rapid speed of change, and the impact these are having on addressing the tough conversations. Then we're going to knuckle down on the friction points that exist within workplaces and provide you with ideas on how to tackle these team gatherings differently.

Riding the wave of change fatigue

There's every chance that you've been through a major change in the past 12 months. It's also highly likely that you will also experience a major change in the coming 12 months either at work or in your life. Not just small changes such as a new process for getting invoices to accounts payable—we're talking about a truly significant shift in what you do and how you do it. The reality is that the role you're doing right now will not be in the same in 12 months' time. Sure, you may have the same job title, but the tasks that make up your day continue to change and reshape themselves based on the rapid environment we live in. The same goes for your team. This constant shift of focus and process in the new world of work can result in something you may have experienced yourself: change fatigue.

Change fatigue happens when an organisation embarks on a change aimed at strategically shifting it in a clear direction and then, along the way, it becomes apparent that it needs to move in a different direction. When people start working in one direction and then suddenly are being asked to throw their weight behind a different objective — often with very little clarity about how, and with minimal resources — motivation can slump badly. With massive change we can often see a polarity between people's reactions and motivations. Why is it some people are completely drained and demotivated by a change event when others — sometimes in the same team — are jumping out of their skin with excitement? In short, it has a lot to do with them having (or not having) a sense of progress. We will address this in some depth throughout this chapter.

Waiting for calm is false hope

The rapid pace of technology and, as we saw in chapter 5, the growth of more remote teams, has fundamentally changed how we do work. These advances are not looking to slow down anytime soon. But that's just one area of change in a much bigger wave. We now live in a VUCA world: one that is more Volatile, Uncertain, Complex and Ambiguous. Waiting for calm among the current chaos is false hope. It's not coming. Despite the fact that our biology riles against this uncertainty, it craves consistency. Therefore, as a leader it's your role to lead among the chaos and to address issues with others amid uncertainty. If you're waiting until things 'settle down' you'll be waiting far too long.

In fact, in a fast-paced working environment, your staff will crave your direction more than ever. The immediacy of feedback in our work has also changed; this is one of the advantages of our current work environments. We can shorten the loops between effort and feedback, creating greater momentum. It's important also to be encouraging effort without immediate reward. With connectivity and the use of cloud-based technology not only can we literally work from anywhere in the world, the lag factor between our work and receiving feedback from others is next to none.

Use this to your advantage. Create a culture of tweaking and iteration rather than working to the grind to produce perfection.

Cultivating an experimentation mindset

Within this rapidly changing environment, the ability of human beings to iterate and experiment is key to staying relevant and current. For example, cloud accounting software company Xero made more than 1000 changes to its online platform over an 18-month period in 2014–15. Its customers would not have noticed many of these changes, but they're all designed for better user experience. It's the pursuit of constant design development and growth that means an organisation stands out from the crowd. Due to the nature of social media we tend to get feedback from customers almost immediately these days, and agile organisations can tweak, change, adapt and update their offering if they choose. The same principles are true in getting feedback from our employees.

Have you ever had a great idea or heard a great way that you could connect with your team, but for some reason it just never took off the way you had hoped it would? Of course you have. The reason why this happens is because when we get a great idea we run with it and immediately try to enforce it as a new ritual — for the best part of a week. But the world gets in the way, doesn't it? A new project is launched, staff go off on leave and the new initiative that we wanted to implement gets put on the backburner, or worse still, discarded completely because we figured 'if it was important enough it would have stuck'.

The way to change this pattern and to not only shift great ideas into habits but to create even better ways of doing things is to shift into a mindset of experimentation. When it comes to leadership science, you don't need to leave scientific thinking up to the scientists. For example, when you hear a great new idea (such as the many that are outlined in this book), think about an experiment that you could undertake using this idea. For example, you may decide to experiment with having individual catch-ups with each of your team once a fortnight. Rather than have this as an open-ended goal, put it into a process such as '10 × 2 × all'—that is, 10 minutes, every fortnight, with every staff member. Then, like a good scientist, start exploring how you can adapt this approach to fit and suit your current context. The things that you could play with are:

- the time of day you have these catch-ups
- the location for the catch-ups (walk and talk meetings, at a café, sitting out in the sunshine)—mix it up
- the topic areas you discuss/address.

A mindset of experimentation is a method that gives you the most objective approach to testing ideas and developing knowledge. Which leader wouldn't want to have robust, evidence-based thinking that is turned into real-world processes with real results? The key in having the tough conversations in a rapid-change environment is to act and be curious about what's happening now instead of waiting for uncertainty.

Let's look at five 'scientist strategies' that will help you approach rapid-change environments with this mindset of experimentation.

Establish an initial hypothesis or hunch

It's important to have something to guide the experiment. Often your initial hunch can be clarified by two simple questions:

- What positive changes may be possible at the end of this experiment?
- If we don't embark on this experiment (and things stay the same) what will happen?

Start to envisage how you think things may work out and the changes that you and your team could make. It's also important, even at this stage, to consider how things could be, but not to be tied to the outcome. Be open to changes happening as part of the process. Having a fuzzy rather than an absolute goal is the aim.

Create a time frame

Experiments aren't open-ended, so create a time frame for people to calibrate their efforts towards. Generally speaking, the shorter the better. Make them sprint...people will rally harder if they can see a finish line. In a busy world with the constant pull of attention in a million different directions, having an experiment that is focused for, say, one to two weeks provides a tight time frame for keeping your eye on the goal. If this short-term experiment shows signs of success, then the testing phase can be lengthened.

Remain curious

As you move through the experiment, maintain a high level of curiosity by constantly thinking, 'Isn't that interesting!', or 'Why did that happen?'. Good scientists are those who are, above all else, fascinated. They're wondering what they may be missing and curious about their own blind spots. Seek to find and gather data by asking the following questions (regardless of whether you believe your experiment is working or not):

- How am I turning up to this task?
- What impact is it having on others?
- Is there another way I could be viewing this?

When you think about it, the world's greatest scientists are constantly searching for answers to a greater challenge they are yet to solve.

See setbacks as learning, not failure

Thomas Edison is famously attributed as saying he didn't fail when prototyping the light bulb—he simply found 10 000 ways not to succeed. Good experiments show us new ways forward even if we're headed in the wrong direction. Too often teams descend into conflict because we place far too much importance on specific success rather than continuing progress. If your team is being pulled into the vortex of defined goals, come back to rule number one: fuzzy goals work best because specific goals tend to only have a binary outcome—we achieved or we didn't. Less-defined goals open up other potential 'green shoots' of ideas because, while you haven't landed at the intended place, your journey will serve as a wonderfully rich experiment.

Share your findings

Research done in the dark is useless. Share your discovery with others. Among your team, provide the opportunity to reflect on how you each approached the experiment, how you may be able to do things differently next time and which aspects worked really well. Beyond that, share it with your peers, fellow work teams and even your wider industry. Your reputation economy will undoubtedly receive a boost if you do.

Worth a watch

In his famous TED Talk, 'Build a tower, build a team', Tom Wujec steps the audience through the 'marshmallow challenge', in which teams receive 18 minutes, 20 pieces of spaghetti, 1 metre of string, 1 metre of sticky tape and a marshmallow with which to create the tallest tower they can. From the thousands of people who have completed this challenge, Tom unpacks some of the key learnings. The most significant learning from this challenge is the power of prototyping. The teams who are the most successful are the ones who test the structure with the marshmallow on the top multiple times. See your actions as prototypes: they are not failures, but an opportunity to test and adapt as you need.

Perhaps you could lead your team through a marshmallow challenge and get them to reflect on the power of prototyping.

By approaching oncoming change through a lens of experimentation you'll navigate uncertainty a whole lot more confidently, but it still won't eliminate conflict; in many cases rapid change brings more conflict to your workspace than any other context. So let's talk about how, as a leader, you can deal with the tough stuff specific to fast change.

Roadblocks: the four ways people respond

When it comes to dealing with conflict and tough conversations it's important to understand how you, and others, respond to rapid change and the roadblocks faced along the way. In our research, we have discovered that there are four ways people respond to roadblocks. As you read through these four ways of responding, consider how the individuals within your team may be responding to rapid change, and also how you can manage these various responses.

Seek opportunities

In every situation lies an opportunity for those who are willing to seek it and act on it. In fact, most small businesses are started because someone was frustrated by a roadblock they hit and decided to do something about it: the mum who starts an organic bamboo clothing line because her child has sensitive skin; the hipster 30-something who opens a coffee shop in their suburb because they couldn't get a piccolo. Most great initiatives in workplaces start out the same way. These are the people who seek out opportunities.

Managing opportunity seekers

Managing those who see possibility and opportunity in a challenge sounds like a dream come true, doesn't it? It's certainly the response to change and roadblocks that you want to see from your team, and what you want to role-model to others. It's this second point that you need to really focus on. All too often we hear risk-averse managers bemoaning their staff because they 'want to do everything yesterday'. Get out of their way! Let them go, and set good guidelines for them. The key to managing an opportunity-seeker is to encourage ideas and ownership while also keeping them focused on getting the 'business as usual' work done.

Be aware and seek

Being aware and seeking is about being aware of change and ripping into what needs to be done in the here and now. This response involves getting real about the current situation and having the conversations that need to be had in order to move forward. The aware-and-seeker is cautiously optimistic and a great person to have in your team.

Managing aware-and-seekers

These people are doers. They are the workers who see a problem and get it sorted straight away. While this works in the moment, this response can be narrow-focused, working only to get through the immediate challenges. The risk is that they may miss opportunities for a new project or a new way of doing the work. Manage this response by encouraging possibility thinking.

Be aware and hide

These are people who are aware that change is here but hide from any action that's required, spending their time instead stressing about the small stuff (such as how to divvy up who orders the coffees for the team in a way that's fair and equitable). These are the worrywarts who seem to disappear from the room during conversations about the topic of change and progress—but they're in your face about everything else.

Managing aware-and-hiders

The frustration in managing this type of response is trying to get people to have a sense of ownership about action. Manage this response by understanding their fears about change, providing clear behavioural steps for the next action and encouraging them to consider alternative perspectives.

See ignorance as bliss

This response is the equivalent of the person who has their head in the sand when change arrives. They float through the days and weeks in ignorant bliss because they fundamentally believe that nothing is really happening differently. These people stick their metaphorical fingers in their ears hoping that simply by ignoring it change will go away.

Managing ignorance-as-blissers

On the plus side, these are the people who keep the work ticking over. Of course, this is only useful if the work they're doing is still relevant in the new environment. If it's not, have the conversations early and deal with resistance to change using the ideas outlined in chapter 7. Remember that if you hear, 'I can't', generally it means either, 'I don't know how to', 'I'm scared to', or 'I don't want to'. Figure out which one it is and address it specifically.

* * *

The key to roadblocks and the four responses that the people around you will elicit is to normalise the response, no matter which of the four they are stuck in. If your conversation with the other person comes across as judgemental, they will resist the change even more. Avoid this by letting them know it's only human to be where they are, and then invite them to see something bigger and better. It doesn't have to stay the way it is forever.

Typically, your tough conversations as a manager will happen with the last two roadblocks, 'be aware and hide' and 'see ignorance as bliss'. In the midst of any tough conversation it's always useful to have a guide. As it turns out, the guide to rapid conflict is in the word itself.

Get RAPID

If you need to have a tough-stuff conversation in the middle of a rapid-change environment, you need to look no further than the acronym RAPID to get it done. This is our five-step fallback guide to managing a tough conversation in the midst of fast-paced change.

Reset

Far too often we try to attack the problem by getting on the front foot early and addressing it directly. This is a great strategy, but trying to address problems derived from chaos in the middle of chaos isn't a smart move. Find the space to hit the reset button. Literally.

Change the space in which you're connecting with others. Embrace the power that our brains have of being refreshed and able to consider new perspectives when we physically move — for example, get into a walk-and-talk habit with your team to hit 'reset' in the middle of a busy day. Maybe it's a meeting room outside your shared workspace, or it's a day off-site with your team. People think differently when they're in a different physical environment. It's a great way to challenge status quo.

Accept

Just for a second, let's try a little game. We want you to respond to a phrase:

Just accept it.

What went through your head? Did you have a response?

Many people don't like the response. Acceptance carries a social stigma. It often feels like giving up. It feels passive, it feels like there's nothing you can do because, really, what's the point, right? Picture the following examples:

- The house you fell in love with went to a higher bidder at auction: you've got to accept it.

- Your organisation is going through a major restructure: you've got to accept it.

- Someone else selfishly ate the last piece of chocolate in the house: you've just got to accept it.

Damn acceptance! It's just giving up. Giving in. Well, maybe not.

There's another side to acceptance. It's not the enemy that it's made out to be. In fact, acceptance — *without judgement* — is the catalyst for action and change. When we accept what's happening, we fully grasp the current situation.

Acceptance doesn't mean doing nothing. Don't get the two confused. Acceptance can actually be quite liberating if you respond in the right way. It's about getting free from the clutches of the past, and getting into action for the possibilities of the future

It's not bad. It's not good. It just is.

From this point of full acceptance, we're able to make a choice about what to do for real, meaningful action. The next time you get frustrated with a decision at work that you have no control over, a project that's not going to plan or a conversation that didn't go as well as you'd hoped, take a couple of deep breaths and accept it. After all, it's hard to change what you don't acknowledge.

Once the situation in front of you is fully grasped, *and accepted*, the actions you take are 100 per cent your responsibility. The point of acceptance may just be the most active thing in the whole process.

Prune

In a busy world, often we simply try to squeeze more in. But having too much time is not one of the problems that your team faces. So if there are new things you want them to be doing, then something has to give. And far too often, existing, entrenched behaviours tend to win out over new behaviours.

So be conscious about finding time and space for new behaviours to flourish in. Remove the clutter of legacy behaviours. Stop before you start.

Fundamentally, the pruning is about acknowledging our limitations. Sport science reminds us that athletes have limitations to physical output: try to push past them and the body shuts down. Similarly, we all have limitations to our energy output—physical, mental, social or work-related. There's a finite amount of energy each person has to allocate each day to thinking, doing, moving, feeling and so on.

Case study: pruning the boss

One example of pruning in action was a session we ran with a senior executive leader, Fiona. If you think your calendar is busy, you should have seen hers! Not only did she run a division of nearly six-hundred people, but her direct report group consisted of more than a dozen people. After going through three major restructures in 18 months, rapid change had taken its toll on the people. It had also taking a toll on Fiona's relationship with her direct reports. But how could she expect them to own change if she couldn't find time to meet with them? So Fiona wanted to prune. Rather than Fiona trying to pick and choose how to prune, we put it in the hands of her direct reports. They looked at her calendar forensically and found her time and space in a number of areas by eliminating, delegating or mitigating certain tasks. Now this 'calendar-up-for-grabs' ritual is being applied to the next layer of leaders in the team. Could you hand your calendar over to your team to do the same?

Intention

Set your intention for how you're going to turn up. Next team meeting, set a clear intention for what you want to achieve or how you need to be. For the next conversation you're planning, set a clear intention about why you're getting together. Clever teams continually check in on the purpose driving their work; and you should too, especially in uncertain times driven by rapid change.

Ask key questions such as:

- Who are we here to serve?
- How will our work make the world a better place?
- How can we take care of each other?
- What's the absolute best use of my time today?

Be courageous about asking these questions. Strangely enough, it's hard to play small and engage in petty behaviour if you're guided by grand intent. Having said that, don't just rest on your intention. It can quickly become lip service unless it's followed up by action.

Define

At the end of the conversation, set a psychological contract about what's coming next by asking the following two questions:

- What are you going to do next?
- What am I going to do next?

Plenty of managers ask the first question, but only the great ones ask the second question. Define the next steps and then make a time to come back together again and check in. Define each other's expectations, and by doing so, you'll build trust along the way.

✳ ✳ ✳

So use RAPID when the heat is on. It will serve you well. But after the final point (Define), it's important to keep motivation high and momentum rolling. The best strategy from this point on is to obsess about progress.

Map it, chunk it, see it

Our colleague and great mate Dr Jason Fox outlines in his book *The Game Changer* the motivating factor that having a strong sense of progress has on human beings. One of the key ways to create a strong sense of progress is to identify where you are now, where you want to be and the steps you need to take to get there.

In workplaces there are various ways that this can be visualised, including project plans, GANNT charts and even the good-old 'to-do' list. But the most important factor is to go visual.

One great example of a way to get visual about direction and behaviours within a team is an approach known as 'scrum'. Jeff Sutherland's book *Scrum* introduces the scrum methodology, whereby groups work in two-week sprints. Jeff's approach is based on short, sharp periods of activity with opportunities to check in and tweak direction. His approach is based on small teams having a wall, board or space with a constant visual reminder of tasks by means of three lists:

- Backlog (ideas of actions for the future—the 'stuff we've gotta get to').
- Doing (the tasks that as a team we are currently working on).
- Done (what has been completed so far in this sprint).

Why is this important when it comes to addressing the tough stuff? Having a visual progress tracker is an accountability tool. It provides a place for you to meet with staff to discuss any differences in understandings and have a candid conversation about which tasks have been completed and why certain tasks haven't been completed to date. The benefit of a whiteboard or a chart is that it provides a strong use of a three-point (see chapter 4) around which to have the conversation. This keeps the conversation about the behaviour rather than about the individual, which is relevant for both one-on-one and team conversations. What we recommend is to grab a whiteboard and get creative.

Conclusion

Rapid change has arrived on most workplaces' doorsteps in recent times and it isn't likely to go away anytime soon. Think about the managers and leaders you admire the most and the qualities they bring. It's often their humanness—their ability to be real—that allows us to connect, but there are times when this is put to the ultimate test. When times are uncertain, volatile and ambiguous, you're not expected to be perfect, and when the world is changing as fast as it is, being perfect today may not serve where you need to be tomorrow. What is critical is your ability to deal with the tough stuff quickly. Flexibility in mindset and a strong sense of humility are the key.

Darren's insights

Personally, I love a rapid-change environment. It provides energy, which ultimately causes a reaction.

Sometimes that energy converts to massive action—momentum towards your goals—and that's exciting stuff. On the other hand, energy from rapid change sometimes causes pressure and friction. But rather than see this as a bad thing, I think it's a wonderful litmus test of our underlying culture.

If conflict does present itself through heady change, especially in the form of heated conflict, it can sometimes indicate something underneath was dysfunctional—perhaps a problematic cultural norm or work process people have continued to suffer through for the sake of status quo. The truth is, it may have been sitting there for a lengthy period of time and the catalyst for it coming to the surface was the change event.

If you think about it through this lens, you're much more likely to welcome and invite change than avoid and resent it—and that can only be a good thing.

Alison's insights

The workplaces that we manage and lead are moving fast, and for me the opportunities that lie ahead are exciting for those prepared to move with them. Now, more than ever, workplaces need to be prepared to embrace their humanness because it's your people who make a difference in a fast work environment. The conversations about culture are prolific in the corporate landscape, although for me it's really just about treating people well and having full permission to be kind. It's not uncommon to hear workplaces talk about love in their values and how they want their employees to feel. I love that!

The thing about building love, though, is that it requires being honest, being real about the things that aren't working and holding people accountable (even when they wish we wouldn't). It requires having the tough conversations and it's these skills that the workplaces of the future will be seeking more than ever.

Sean's insights

I am also in love with rapid change, high pressure and dealing with uncertainty. For me it is stimulating and exciting, a reason to do something new, to pour more energy into the next challenge. However, I have also had to learn the hard way that these intense environments uncover our limitations as human beings, particularly the limits imposed by our biology. What I know from my research in elite performance environments teeming with fast-paced, high-pressure change is that you have to look after your number one resource: energy! It's time to move away from the whole time-management conversation and start talking about how to manage personal energy. In fact, calling time a resource is a misnomer. It's not a resource, it's a constraint—energy is a resource. If you want to build a high-performance team in a rapid-change environment, you're going to have to extract maximum effort from all of your team members, so it's crucial that they develop the tools to manage energy optimally. Drive them hard, but balance it with opportunity for adequate recovery, and watch them thrive in this new world of chaos!

Chapter summary

- Change fatigue is what people experience when organisations shift focus rapidly without any consistency of direction, with limited resources and at the cost of progress. It can be avoided.

- You don't have to be a scientist to think in terms of experiments and adaptions. Leaders who view what they do with an experimentation mindset are more open to tweaking and changing as needed.

- Understand the four ways that people respond to roadblocks and encourage possibility thinking without judgement

- Get RAPID: find ways to hit Reset; Accept things as they are actively; Prune the unnecessary; set a new Intent in the new landscape; and Define the next steps from here.

- Progress, not perfection, is the goal.

- Find ways to get visual so that you can track progress and have the tough conversations when progress is halted.

GREAT LEADERS
help others to see
OPPORTUNITY
in ADVERSITY.

9

DEALING WITH THE ROUGH STUFF
The big three: restructure, redundancy and dismissal

People get attached to their roles at work. Their job becomes an identity for some, and ownership for others, and for some their job may even go a long way to defining who they are. As a result, restructure, redundancy, dismissal or personal injury or illness can have a major impact on individuals due to profound feelings of grief and loss.

Psychiatrist and best-selling author Elisabeth Kübler-Ross pioneered the understanding of the stages of grief and loss for the health sector, and in many ways turned an entire culture around. Before Kübler-Ross's work, hospital staff, including doctors, were ordered to never discuss death or even the possibility of it with their patients. The results of this misguided practice, particularly for terminally ill patients, were shocking. Patients felt loneliness, frustration and a lack of humanity as they endured their last days on earth. Thankfully, Kübler-Ross's work brought about change and has made the health system significantly better for it.

Unfortunately, the corporate world still works like a 1950's hospital. We don't talk about the big three: restructure, redundancy and dismissal; we don't talk about the pain and disruption they cause—but we should. We need to map grief and loss better when people's work worlds are tipped on their head. It's time for change.

Mapping the journey

Change is a constant within the workplace, but the extent of disruption created by restructures, redundancies or dismissals warrants a closer look. These disruptions bring with them inevitable tough conversations, uncertainty and disorder. As a manager and a leader, it is often your role to be seen as being in control, and yet the decisions are often out of your control, and you have to maintain a semblance of balance between chaos and confidence. This chapter explores some ways of navigating through this rough terrain.

This rough stuff is big and causes significant emotional upheaval, but the big three all have one thing in common: transition—a passage or journey from one form, state, style, place, context or *reality* to another.

Before we get specific about how we can employ strategies to help us manage the rough stuff with our staff, it is worth exploring the transition process in some greater depth.

The common denominator: transition

We deal with transitions every day: from being asleep to being awake, from leaving home to entering the workplace, from being with others to being alone. Certainly, these transitions are smaller and less challenging than the three rough-stuff challenges explored in this chapter, but the fundamental principles remain the same. According to developmental psychologist Richard Harmer, who specialises in helping executives and organisations find their purposeful leadership, all transitions have a start, a middle and an end. He defines them in the following way:

- *Start.* First, we have to acknowledge that one reality is ending and that certain roles, expectations, perspectives, responsibilities and benefits or challenges are likely to end with it.

- *Middle.* Second, in letting go of this (now old) reality, there will probably be a feeling that something is missing, which may result in you feeling both concerned by the uncertainty and excited by the new possibilities.

- *End.* Finally, there is the creation or embracing of a new beginning or reality with all of the roles, perspectives, responsibilities and benefits/challenges that come with this new experience.

The process of transition is shown in figure 9.1.

Figure 9.1: Richard Harmer's model of the process of transition

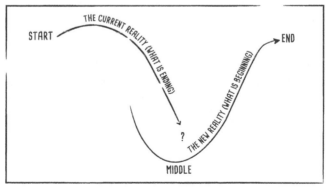

Mindset makes a difference

There is something else common to all transitions: the attitude or mindset that is brought to the experience. The mindset that a person chooses to adopt during times of transition is the key to coping or not coping. As a manager, your ability to influence the mindsets of others is also crucial to successful transitions. Let's explore further the role of mindsets.

We have all been there: the sense of hurt and loss at no longer feeling as if you're in the driver's seat of your work or career. In our experience, more than 80 per cent of people who have experienced transition, by a change in role or responsibility at work (through restructure), losing their job (through redundancy or dismissal) or no longer being able to do their job (through injury or illness), have been happier and more satisfied six months after they commenced the transition journey than they were at the start. That is a massive percentage and far greater than we would have expected. The 80 per cent who were happier were those who adopted a more positive mindset during the experience—especially in the start and middle phases of the transition.

You may be thinking, 'That sounds all well and good for you guys, but I am in the middle of this transition journey right now. How can I stay positive when I'm faced with so much uncertainty about my future?'

We agree. We felt the same when we were in the middle of it too.

Here are some of the things that work, regardless of where you are in the transition journey. These suggestions are designed to build on what you already know, open up a space of possibilities for new opportunities to be created for you and by you, and provide you with the confidence to create an energising pathway towards your new post-transition reality. Our suggestions fall into the following three actions:

- Talk yourself up: it's all about translation.
- Hit the pause button: it's all about relaxation.
- Create the pathway to your new reality: it's all about adaptation.

Figure 9.2 shows how the transition model might change when new mindsets are used.

Figure 9.2: building the mindsets for successful transitions

Talk yourself up: it's all about translation

Taking the best of your past and what you really enjoy doing and repurposing it to support, inspire and enable you (and others!) to create your new reality is at the core of translation. It's about doing a personal and professional audit, and working out what you really want to do and what you're good at; letting go of the old, owning your strengths and talking up your passions, perspectives and performance within the new reality in which you find yourself. These are the four steps of translation.

Step one is taking some time to look for the best in your past experiences and successes. Ask yourself:

- What do I really enjoy about the work that I do and what am I really good at?

- What comes naturally to me and what feedback from others have I received that reinforces this?

- What knowledge, skills, experiences and attributes do I have, and what successes have I had in my career using these?

- What aspects of my previous roles have I been really passionate about?

In step two, you need to let go of all of those aspects of your current job and behaviours that no longer serve you as you work to create your new reality. Ask yourself:

- What are the aspects of my previous role or roles that I did not enjoy and no longer want to do?
- What attitudes or mindsets do I hold at present that are not useful to me as I commence this transition journey?

In step three, you need to own up to your strengths. We often downplay our strengths because we don't want to appear overly confident or arrogant to others. But, in times of transition these social rules don't apply. We no longer have to try to fit in with others—after all, we're no longer going to be working with the same people. Now is the time to own what you're good at. You have to fully believe your own hype for others to do so!

In step four, talk up your passions and performance. There is a really basic law in psychology that explains much of human behaviour: we're attracted towards what makes us feel good and we avoid what makes us feel bad. Simply put, we pursue pleasure and avoid pain.

The same goes when translating your old reality into the new reality you're creating. Talk up what you're passionate about to get others excited about you and what you can do for them. Also, showcase your past performances to others. Think about the last time you went to look at a new car in the showroom. The salesperson would have quickly identified your basic needs in a new car, and would then have talked up the performance aspects of the car they were selling in ways that matched your needs. Talk up your past performances in ways that address the current dilemmas of your new audience.

Hit the pause button: it's all about relaxation

Often we start the transition journey feeling exhausted. We've either been feeling stressed or worried in the lead-up to the transition we now face, or we've been working to our limits just trying to keep all of the balls in the air in a situation that had become untenable.

When we start the transition journey—and especially when we're in the middle phase—we may experience emotions that often arise when we're uncertain about our own and others' future. This is a natural experience (part of the pursuit of pleasure, avoidance of pain rule mentioned earlier).

In these situations we often try to force a decision or a solution: 'If I could just get some clarity about the situation, I would know what to do next!' Obviously every person's situation is different. If possible, however, avoid rushing into the next role or job. Take some time. Slow down. Hit the pause button. Try something new. For example, read a book from a genre different from your usual preferences, talk to different people, get out of your daily routine, watch different television programs or spend some time alone in new surroundings.

Why? It's hard to create a new vision for how you would like your new reality to be if you don't have any new experiences to feed into this new vision. If you fail to have new experiences you may find yourself recreating aspects of your old world that you wanted to let go of. And, more importantly, you should get some rest and relaxation before commencing the next leg of your career journey.

Create the pathway to your new reality: it's all about adaptation

Imagine that you are at the edge of a vast plain and on the horizon you see a distinctive landmark that acts as a signpost to your ideal future—your new world. There is no obvious pathway to this destination. What do you do? Obviously, you start walking. And in so doing you forge a path to your destination.

The passage of transition is often like this. We are often explorers of what can feel like uncharted territory. We need to improvise, experiment and adapt our way towards our new reality. Learn by doing. Try something, then measure your progress, refine your approach and try again. Create the map to your new world through the journey itself.

There is no single perfect way to traverse the unknown. Perseverance, self-belief and personal dedication are all aspects of yourself that you have at your disposal.

Some other important activities you should add to your travel pack for the journey include the following:

- *Be true to yourself.* What's the point of journeying to your new world if along the way you lose a connection with who you are, what you stand for and what you're deeply passionate about?

- *Create a compelling vision of the new reality you are heading towards and make it high definition.* Remember the pursuit of pleasure, avoidance of pain rule we spoke about earlier? Your vision for what you want to experience in the new world needs to be compelling enough to you (and those important to you) to risk leaving the safety of your current reality in order to obtain it.

- *Experiment, improvise and adapt your way through the terrain to the new world.* A mindset of experimentation is critical when you're trying new things. We're not likely to get it perfect first time (if at all!). Sure, we want to enjoy the journey as much as possible, but in the game we call transition it's the end that counts. Lay your foundations deep, build rewarding and supporting relationships, ask the questions that make you tremble, dance with the unknown, trust that the way forward will become clear to you, say yes to opportunities that you feel will help you make progress, proceed until apprehended — and then proceed some more.

- *Celebrate your successes — both great and small.* We get so fixated on the end result that we fail to notice and celebrate our successes (however small they may feel) along the way. However, these celebrations are important in sustaining the transition journey. They are like markers indicating progress along our journey. They also provide us with a point to return to if we feel we have become lost somewhere along the way. Celebrate alone. Celebrate with others. Celebrate often!

In the discipline of psychology there has been extensive research into the factors that underpin successful transitions. According to clinical psychologist Charles Snyder, author of *The Psychology of Hope: You Can Get There from Here*, one important factor in navigating life and career transitions effectively is the psychological condition of hope. Snyder describes hope as having two key elements: the first element is willpower, which he defines as self-belief and a willingness to be the agent of your own destiny; and the second element is 'waypower', which he describes as a clear vision of a desired future, coupled with a clear pathway towards it.

Richard Harmer offers a third element, which he calls 'wantpower', for dealing with the rough stuff: regardless of the situations or circumstances we may find ourselves in, each of us has boundless persistence and tenacity to follow the path towards what we're truly passionate about. Staying connected to your 'wantpower' when dealing with the rough stuff (and helping others to do the same) will result in creating an experience of transition that can be liberating rather than scary. Perhaps you have had someone say to you, 'Changing jobs was the best thing that ever happened to me'—essentially they are saying, 'I have made the transition'.

Gaining a better understanding of transitions and how they affect us (and our staff) is a cornerstone for handling the big three conversations well. Gaining a level of empathy (see chapter 7) is a powerful tool in these rough-stuff conversations. By examining your own reactions to transitions, you become attuned to others undertaking their own transition. Let's now look at how we, as managers and leaders, can specifically deal with the rough stuff of restructure, redundancy and dismissal.

Moments of truth: having the termination conversation

Conversations about termination are often called moments of truth for a leader of others: because of redundancy or dismissal you are now in a position where you are called upon to terminate a member of your team. Time to take a deep breath.

This conversation requires high levels of emotional sensitivity, as well as courage. Interestingly, the word 'courage' is taken from the Latin word *cor*, which means 'heart'. So, this is a good place to start when you need to have a rough-stuff conversation to end someone's tenure in your organisation. Monitor your heart rate. When your heart is racing, it usually means you are stressed, worried or even scared. These emotions are completely natural for the situation you are facing. One quick technique when you notice your heart racing is to start to count the beats. How many are there? In your mind, try to get your heart to beat at the same time you take a breath, or close enough to it. In matching your heart rate with your rate of breath, you naturally slow down both, which will result in you feeling calmer and more focused.

When preparing for a rough-stuff conversation involving termination, you need to do four essential things:

- prepare yourself
- keep it real
- stay on message
- maintain the other person's self-esteem.

Prepare yourself

If you can, take some time to prepare yourself for the conversation. What do you need to do in order to remain as relaxed, attentive and empathic as possible? This may mean having a good night's sleep the night before, or talking the conversation through with a trusted (and objective) colleague, or having some time by yourself immediately prior to the conversation to calm your thoughts and ground yourself. Whatever you need to do to connect with your courage, boost your emotional sensitivity and remain true to yourself and your message, do it.

You need to be centred and grounded within yourself for your rough-stuff conversation to be the same.

Keep it real

Remember that you're going to have a conversation that will result in the other person feeling like they are losing control of their present situation. And when people feel like they are losing control, they can react in some unpredictable ways. For example, they can get defensive or angry, or upset or quiet.

The most important thing for you to do is provide the person with all the information they need to make some informed choices about what the decision means to them. Often we sugar-coat the message to the person receiving it because we're trying to look out for them, and sometimes even protect ourselves, but this disempowers both of you. Be real. Tell them how it is. Include the facts of the situation as well as the relevant details of what, when, how and whatever else. You may even like to write down the answers to these key points for yourself in preparation for your conversation.

For people to make informed choices about their future life and career, they need to be aware of the reality of their present situation.

Stay on message

Following on from being real, make sure you stay on message. As we mentioned before, when people feel like they are losing control (fast!) they can act in unpredictable ways—they may want to enter into a debate with you about the relative merits of your decision, or bargain with you about lifting their game in return for not being terminated.

Imagine you are in a carriage on a set of railway tracks. Either side of the railway tracks is a swamp. Imagine that the place where the tracks meet the horizon is your objective and the carriage you are standing in is your key message. In reality, if you were facing this scenario, the safest and smoothest place for you to be would be in the carriage and on the tracks. Rough-stuff conversations are just like this: if you stray into the swamp it can get a little bumpy. Ask yourself these questions:

- What is the outcome I want *for me* from this conversation?

- What is the outcome I want *for the other person* involved in this conversation?

- Given the outcomes, what are the three key messages I want the other person to take from the conversation?

- What am I not prepared to discuss with the other person as part of the conversation?

Know and stick to your desired outcome and key messages to ensure your rough-stuff conversation stays on track.

Maintain the other person's self-esteem

In delivering the messages of your rough-stuff conversation and ending a person's tenure in your organisation, you will be challenging their feelings of self-worth. In these conversations, you play an important role in helping to maintain the person's self-esteem so they leave the conversation thinking: 'I am upset by the message, but my manager was really good about it'.

In our experience, if you follow the three points we have already mentioned for conducting a rough-stuff conversation you will, by default, maintain the other person's self-esteem. A good rule of thumb is to imagine yourself in the other person's shoes and remember to offer the words you would most like to hear, in ways that are also true to the situation they face, as well as being aligned to your desired outcomes and key messages.

A good mantra to adopt is to offer hope and a way forward from your rough-stuff conversations.

True transparency: give them 100 per cent

In a situation such as a restructure, respecting others enough to tell them 100 per cent of what you know is the art of true transparency. Remember, it's not your role to own others' emotions. Imagine if you changed the reality for someone in your team by not telling them the full picture. This clearly says that, as a manager, I don't think you can handle the real situation. Or worse still, that I can't handle your potential anger. It's only ever half the story if you only tell half of what you know. Likewise, it's always 100 per cent of the story if you tell everything that you know.

Management and leadership practices that are based on espionage or on, 'Let's hold it back until ...' are relics of a long-gone era around military models where keeping your next move under wraps was important. When it comes to restructures, the keep-quiet strategy—the strategy that says, 'Let's do it all in the room and hold it back for six months and then go "Ta da! Here it is"'—needs to be rethought. We've been unable to find any research that suggests this process actually works. Often it's the result of an executive team being scared of its own emotions and fearing it will not be able to handle the fallout.

It's never your job as a leader or a manager of people to determine their future. It's their choice. Whether they want to leave or want to stay, you can't chain them to the desk. In fact, if they feel as though you have done just that, guess what they're going to do? Pick the lock. When we communicate our message clearly, openly and transparently, the vast majority of people say they would prefer to be informed of a restructure or a potential restructure. Even if it upsets them, they would rather know, so that they can deal with it, than be kept in the dark.

Case study: Waldo

Waldo is the manager of a team of 10. He gets on well with his team and, in turn, his team largely achieves its set tasks and budgets.

Waldo has just come out of a heads-of-sections meeting, where he found out his department is facing wide-reaching restructures. At this stage he is not sure who will be affected, or even if it will affect his team at all.

Managers are encouraged to discuss this with their teams, but Waldo and a few other managers have decided not to discuss the possibility of change with their staff at this stage, as they want to gather more information before letting people know what is happening.

When questioned about why he isn't telling his staff about this issue, he replies, 'I don't want to tell them half the story. I want to let my staff know the whole picture and not cause them any undue stress or worry, particularly if it doesn't even affect us'.

Reflections on Waldo's decision

Here Waldo is making assumptions about the behaviour of his team and taking away their ownership and ability to make decisions by changing reality—in this case, by withholding this information and not telling them about the restructure upfront.

(continued)

Case study: Waldo *(cont'd)*

When we unpacked Waldo's decision-making with him in a coaching session what we found was that his decision came from three key areas:

- *Waldo loved his staff.* He had great positive regard for the people who worked for him and he had a genuine affection for them and the work that they did. It manifested itself in a parental style of leadership, where he cared about them so much that he wanted to protect them, and one way he thought he could protect them was by not telling them the bad news.

- *Waldo loved being an expert.* Right through his life he had been great at school, he had been great at his job and he had been a great manager. He's the type of guy who would give you an awesome answer any time you took a problem to him. And here he was being asked to communicate something that he didn't have expertise in and which was threatening to his identity.

- *Waldo loved to be loved.* His ego was at play. Ego's not a bad thing, but it can get in the road of certain things. Waldo loved that his staff liked him and thought he was a good manager. It made him feel good and here he was in a situation where he could be the bearer of bad news and they would think less of him, which was very threatening.

Waldo's decision was coming from good places, but inherently it had an egocentric origin, rather than one focused on his team. Waldo walked away from the coaching session having realised his intention to withhold information from staff was driven by his own insecurities and fears, and that if he gave in to these feelings he would have been potentially undoing trustful working relationships with staff that in some cases he had built over close to a decade.

By respecting others enough to give them all the information, Waldo effectively empowered his staff, and in doing so, opened up the lines of communication, which was critical for mapping the transitions in the restructure.

Stepping through grief and loss

At the heart of change, individuals often feel a sense of grief and loss—loss of a hoped-for future, grief over changed relationships with others, and the loss of a job and financial security. Elisabeth Kübler-Ross's work on the stages of grief provides a useful framework for understanding the emotional journey that we and others go through when faced with grief and loss as experienced through restructure, redundancies, dismissal, or personal injury or illness.

Kübler-Ross's model outlines five stages that individuals go through in the process of dealing with grief and loss. The extent to which an individual experiences each stage and the length of time it may take them to move through a stage varies greatly. If people are particularly stuck in going through the transition, this model can be useful to consider.

According to Kübler-Ross, the five stages of grief are:

- denial
- anger
- bargaining
- depression
- acceptance.

The denial stage

In the denial stage people are likely to say things such as, 'I feel fine', and 'This can't be happening to me'.

Denial is usually only a temporary defence for the individual, and it's usually replaced by a heightened awareness of the impact of the change on them and their family.

Ways to manage this stage include the following:

- Provide a forum for questions if they come up.
- Communicate the message consistently and through various media.
- Let people know clearly what the next step is.

The anger stage

In the anger stage people are likely to say things such as, 'Why me? It's not fair!', 'How can this happen to me?', and 'Who is to blame?'

Once they are in the second stage, they recognise that denial can't continue.

Ways to manage this stage include the following:

- Depersonalise the situation (go back to the strategies offered in chapters 4 and 6).

- Direct the conversation towards solutions rather than problems.

- Rather than focus on what the end step will be, just focus on what the next step needs to be.

The bargaining stage

In the bargaining stage people are likely to say things such as, 'I'll do anything to keep my job', and 'I will take a pay cut if...'

The third stage involves the hope that the individual can somehow postpone or delay the change. Psychologically, the individual is saying, 'I understand this change is going to happen, but if I could just do something to buy more time...'

Ways to manage this stage include the following:

- Be clear on what can't be changed.

- Encourage the possibility mindset that comes from this stage — there may be a viable solution that you hadn't considered.

- Link people up with supports, resources and websites that may be relevant.

The depression stage

In the depression stage people are likely to say things such as, 'I'm so sad, why bother with anything?', 'This is the only job I know. What's the point?', and 'Who else will give me a chance?'

During the fourth stage, the person begins to understand the certainty of change. For this reason they may start to disconnect with the workplace and their relationships there.

Ways to manage this stage include the following:

- Show empathy and understanding for what they're experiencing.
- Reconnect people with hope by exploring other times when they have successfully navigated change.
- Allow time for grief and loss to be processed.

The acceptance stage

In the acceptance stage, people are likely to say things such as, 'It's going to be okay', and 'I can't fight it, so I may as well prepare for it'.

In this last stage, people begin to come to terms with the change and are more open to what the future holds.

Ways to manage this stage include the following:

- Guide people into action. Action precedes clarity and helps with making decisions about the future.
- Provide assistance to plan future options.
- Support their choices.

Gaining a greater understanding of the stages of grief and loss is important for any manager or leader who is mapping staff through the rough stuff. For example, when you're managing a team undergoing restructure, be a little forensic with each member of your team. Where is each individual within the stages of grief and loss? Are some angry? Perhaps some may be deflated, whereas others are eager to move on. Each individual stage requires specific strategies—get clear to get the best out of the transition you and your staff are going through.

Disruption creates innovation

Restructures, redundancies, dismissals and personal injury or illness can all create seismic disruptions to the workplace. One of the side effects of disruption at work is the need to do things differently. What worked before may not work in this changed landscape. Leading organisations are going out of their way to actually create disruption at work because they recognise that through disruption innovations are born. Once people have reached a stage of acceptance, they find ways to embrace and capitalise on the disruption and chaos. Consider what may be possible that we had never thought of doing before. This is where thought leaders are born.

Disruptions have a way of shaking up our lives and getting us to consider these questions: 'What do I really want to be doing?' and 'What is really important to me?' Consider the employee who has been in the same job for 10 years, not hating it but not loving it either. Being faced with restructure or redundancy may be the big jolt that gets them to finally pursue the career they have always wanted.

When faced with the transitions that are created by the big three, consider how the future may be better because of this experience. Consider the following useful questions:

- What things are possible in this changing landscape that I hadn't considered before?

- What have I put off that I now may be able to achieve?

- What if we were to get rid of _____? What would happen then?

- Who could I connect with who would give me a fresh outside perspective on this situation?

Conclusion

The level of disruption created by the big three—restructure, redundancy and dismissal—is major. It's often your role as manager to be the messenger, to be seen as being in control and responsible for things that are totally outside of your control, but talking through the pain, disruption and frustration of the big three is often not as scary as we think.

Taking the time to walk alongside others through these transitions will support both them and you to navigate the rough terrain. Be true to yourself, celebrate the successes and instil hope for what may be possible in the future. What could come out of these experiences may be better than anything you had imagined.

Darren's insights

It's time to put a stop to the outdated processes that many large organisations use in downsizing and restructuring. It generally looks like this: the board or executive team makes a decision to downsize or restructure the workforce, then they swear each other to secrecy as plans are carefully crafted before the big announcement.

This works poorly in theory and even more poorly in practice. For starters, this never stays under wraps in the boardroom: information leaks. People are smart and can see changes coming well before they are announced, so by the time D-day does approach, the announcement is met by a cynical, distrustful workforce who resist change actively. It simply doesn't work.

Executives, like anyone else, feel emotions, and the predominant emotion present when thinking about withholding potentially upsetting news is a fear-based response: 'We're worried about what staff might do'; 'We're worried staff might react negatively'; 'We're worried about our profits'. Smart leaders don't give in to fear at times of restructure; they rise above it.

Alison's insights

Having worked in vocational rehabilitation for a number of years, supporting the return to work of individuals after illness and injury, I have seen that life's biggest disruptions can also be the birthplace of life's greatest triumphs.

I once worked closely with a builder whose whole identity was connected to what he did. His world fell apart when he was told he couldn't work anymore because of a back injury.

When I met him six months later, he had embarked upon an amazing transition — his whole life had changed. He had moved through the rough stuff and was now employed fulltime as a real estate agent. He was loving the job and his new boss was loving him; his future had never looked brighter. He looked at me with tears in his eyes and said, 'Thank you. I wish I had done this years ago'. Going through the rough stuff is what allows us to see a future that we had never considered possible.

Sean's insights

When it comes to emotional responses to change and transition, don't you sometimes just feel like yelling, 'Oh, would ya just get over it!' at the top of your lungs? After all, you are a manager and it's not your job to sort out people's personal, emotional reactions to stuff that is just part of life in business. However, we also know that doing nothing to acknowledge and support people during big changes can lead to rifts and tensions that can undermine an organisation.

There is a middle path to tread here: when leading people through the big three challenges, instead of ignoring the human issues or jumping in to psychoanalyse staff, you will get good results if you simply open up to people with a non-judgemental mindset. Acknowledge the grief and emotional difficulties as totally normal, human responses. You don't have to fix personal difficulties—you just have to let the people know that they have your support.

Chapter summary

- Be okay with anger. It's just a part of the grief and loss process, and people will move through it quickly.

- Ensure that you give a clear and consistent message to all parties. If the goal posts change, communicate this as soon as possible.

- When dealing with staff who may be in the bargaining phase, be clear about what's negotiable and what's not.

- Set clear boundaries and expectations, and then trust others to make choices for themselves.

- As a manager you may also be affected by a restructure or redundancies in the same way that your staff are. Be authentic to your own experience, too.

- Invest time and energy in your people: this is the key to supporting others through transitions.

- Great leaders instil a sense of hope for a better future. In the middle of uncertainty, find ways to provide hope.

Make
YOURSELF
part of the solution
RATHER THAN
PART OF THE
PROBLEM.

10

DEALING WITH THE BLUFF STUFF

Handling emotional manipulation in the workplace

In the workplace—as in a good poker game—there are players who have mastered the art of the bluff stuff. Their behaviours and the words they use are inconsistent, toxic, manipulative and undermining. Trying to spot when they are bluffing and when they are playing straight can be exhausting.

Emotional manipulation within the workplace is a hot topic. It's such a hot topic that it's the subject of numerous books that cover the issue in far greater depth than we will attempt in one chapter. But be certain that some of the toughest conversations you could face in the workplace may be the result of emotional manipulation at play.

Emotional manipulation in the workplace has left a number of casualties in its wake, and some of the greatest casualties have been staff morale, employee engagement, productivity and customer satisfaction. It's critical, as with all tough situations, to address the bluff stuff. Any situation that results in you or others feeling intimidated or shamed at work is unacceptable.

To help you get your head around the bluff stuff, we will examine the two types of perpetrators of these behaviours, the behaviours they exhibit and your role as a manager in reinforcing versus shutting down these behaviours. We will also provide a deeper understanding of effective strategies for dealing with the different manifestations of emotional manipulation.

Two kinds of bluffers

It's important to first distinguish between different types of bluffers. In any workplace there are two key kinds of emotional manipulators: the ones that do it with malicious intent (snakes in suits), and the ones that don't (damaged survivors). Both kinds are driven to get their own way at almost any cost. They can be toxic in the work environment and are damaging to the people around them. Nonetheless, the differences between the two kinds of manipulators mean they require quite different responses.

Snakes in suits

The first kind of bluffer—a psychopathic personality—is the poster child for intentional, cold-blooded, purpose-driven, emotional manipulation. Renowned expert on psychopathy Dr Robert Hare and organisational psychologist Dr Paul Babiak called their book—in which they describe the psychopaths in the business world—*Snakes in Suits*. According to Hare and Babiak, psychopaths exhibit a cluster of distinctive personality traits, the most significant of which is an utter lack of conscience. The psychopath has no sense of guilt to convince themselves to put the brakes on a hurtful approach, and no conscience to worry about the collateral damage created by the relentless pursuit of their personal goals. They also have huge egos, short tempers and an appetite for excitement.

Psychopaths appear to be missing some frontal lobe functionality in the brain that processes emotion and creates feelings of guilt and empathy. So, the question the psychopath asks is not, 'Why would I want to do something that could hurt this person?'. When it suits their purpose, the question is, 'Why not?'. Psychopaths are often smart: they understand the rules and find ways to subvert them. They tend to focus on what they can get away with, preying on the vulnerable, and will relentlessly take advantage of a person or situation if given the chance. Part of the challenge of trying to deal with a psychopath is that, because they don't feel guilt, they will have no issue with lying their way out of a jam, straight to your face, in circumstances in which you could not imagine a normal person lying.

Have you ever had an interaction with a colleague, boss or direct report in the workplace that left you feeling bad about yourself, and about your role in contributing to a poor outcome, even though you knew you weren't responsible? Maybe you were being held accountable for a report that you were never told you had to submit in the first place. Perhaps you delegated a task to someone and had been assured the job was taken care of, only to discover it has been neglected and now you are the only one to blame. Somehow even you start to feel convinced that you are solely culpable for the unacceptable results, even though there is no way that you could be. Furthermore, the person who should be responsible has convinced everyone else that they are a victim in the whole mess. If so, you may have been dealing with a psychopath.

How to spot a psychopath in your workplace

Spotting a psychopath is not an easy thing to do. It's estimated that there is one in every 100 people, and the ratio can increase as you climb the corporate ladder. We defer to Hare and Babiak's advice on psychopathic behaviours to watch out for at work, and have summarised their insights overleaf.

- *They are happy to invite you to their pity party.* Psychopaths have no problem frequently asking for your forgiveness—coming up with countless reasons for poor behaviour or performance, only to repeat the same behaviour just after securing your pity.

- *They often display emotional incongruence.* They don't show emotion when you would expect most people to, such as when someone has genuinely been hurt or injured, or they display an emotion that doesn't fit the situation, such as laughing about someone else's unfortunate circumstances.

- *They act as parasites.* Psychopaths will excessively delegate to others, and often not put in much effort of their own, taking the credit for others' successes and assigning blame for their own failures.

- *They practise crafty deception.* They have no problem telling a lie, but are smart enough to seed it with a grain of truth so that they can always defend their position.

- *They pour on the charisma when it works for them.* You will know psychopaths as people who set out to charm everyone in the office as long as it gets them what they want. They can quickly drop a person from their buddy list any time that person is no longer needed.

- *They overtly display arrogance.* Psychopaths don't mind talking themselves and their deeds up—quite a bit.

- *They deflect responsibility.* They will never accept blame and are pretty good at conjuring up evidence to show that it's someone else's fault.

- *They frequently take risks.* You won't see these guys hang around too long at the dull, repetitive work; they will be the ones stretching the company boundaries, most likely in questionable ways.

- *They relentlessly pursue power.* Psychopaths appear to have a thirst for climbing the ladder that's more about the status of the position than it is about the opportunity to make positive changes or to do good for the company.

This list is a good start, but we remind you that no single characteristic or behaviour outlined is an indicator that you're dealing with a psychopath. Just because someone you know fits one or two of the behavioural descriptors doesn't mean that they are a psychopath. We suggest it's worth leaving it to the experts to do the full diagnosis. Nonetheless, it can be helpful to count the number of red flags for psychopathy that are evident in a person, and put yourself on alert when you start to see a cluster forming around multiple descriptors from this list. For example, you may have had a direct report look you in the eye and acknowledge that it's their job to follow up with a key client. When you find out the client has been neglected, the direct report nonchalantly claims either that they did indeed follow up with the client (a lie) and somehow the client is unreliable, or that they delegated the responsibility to someone else on the team, who didn't follow through on the request (also a lie). The psychopath won't stop there, however. They will probably come up with some vague, unverifiable evidence, albeit interwoven with a grain of truth, such as recalling a water-cooler conversation with their colleague where they had asked the colleague indirectly for help on the client follow-up. In talking about the circumstances, they demonstrate a flatness of emotion, which would be unexpected given the seriousness of the issue.

Simply, the experience may have felt like you were caught in a web of confusing stories, strange behaviours and disconcerting emotional responses, coming from someone at work who seemed rather unattached about the whole affair, even though it was hugely important to the business.

What to do about the suited snake

For true psychopaths, there's little hope of sustainable behaviour change because their brains are hardwired differently from yours. Hare and Babiak tell us that psychopaths in prison don't have any hope for rehabilitation, and it's probably no different in the corporate world. The biggest mistake you can make in dealing with a psychopath is to get trapped in their world. If you try to figure them out through your own lens of being a normal human being, with intact emotions (particularly around guilt), and if you put energy into trying to change or fix them, you'll face nothing but frustration, disbelief and anxiety. Hare and Babiak remind us that there isn't much you can do about these scary individuals, but it's also good to acknowledge that it's not your fault if you have tried and failed to make a difference with them. It appears that the best strategies for responding to psychopaths are generally pretty basic:

- If you can identify one, don't hire them in the first place.

- Refrain from engaging with them where possible.

- Set strong personal and professional boundaries when working with them.

- Let go of any expectations of normality and any hope of making sense of their behaviour.

Damaged survivors

The second type of emotional manipulator can sometimes be nearly as difficult as the psychopath, but not quite. Like psychopaths, this second group of bluffers often have a singular focus—to get what they want—and they will also hurt people along the way. In their case, however, the harm they cause is usually a result of ignorance of the impact of their actions (borne out of self-absorption) rather than the evil intent we see in the psychopath. On a positive note, they do have the power to change, and if you understand their behaviour patterns, and apply some of the tools of the tough-stuff conversations, you may get more traction with them than previously. At least you can learn to depersonalise their often offensive communication and, at best, you may actually connect with them in a way that allows for a completely different, more effective conversation.

For the most part, these are people who don't intend to hurt others directly, but are so caught up in their own (usually insecure) worlds that they act without much empathy and apparent care. Unlike the hardwiring of the psychopath, this group's behaviour has most often been shaped by personally challenging experiences, particularly during the formative years of their lives. They may have experienced bullying as a child, had emotionally or physically abusive parents or other people of influence around them, survived some traumatic situations or had intimidating role models in their lives. These people are more common than your average psychopath. Most of us have known a boss, employee or customer who fits this category (and maybe you find yourself here during crisis times as well). There can be a range of types of manipulators, from those who tend to be passive–aggressive and incite guilt trips, to those who rule by intimidating and shaming.

What distinguishes the damaged survivor from the psychopath is that they will experience guilt at some point (although you may not always see it), they can show genuine glimmers of empathy, and they will respond to effective coaching intervention if they are open to and commit to it.

An example of the damaged survivor at work is the person who tears a strip off a colleague for a small oversight, say for minor spelling errors in a proposal, making the person feel about as small as a flea, but then genuinely praises them for a job well done the next day. You may also experience these people as mean, uncompromising hard-asses at work, but observe that they are caring philanthropists outside work.

Most of the rest of this chapter will be dedicated to dealing with this second type of manipulator, the damaged survivor. For this type of bluffer, we maintain that there's goodness in the person somewhere, and it may come out over time, if you can disarm the thick, protective outer layer that repels your normal attempts to engage and has them on the offensive much of the time. Let's look at some effective strategies for dealing with bluff stuff from the damaged survivor who unintentionally hurts and bullies people along the way.

Two-way street

The first strategy for dealing with the bluff stuff is to take responsibility for your part in it. Emotional manipulation is a two-way street. When faced with this type of destructive manipulation and behaviour, you always have choices, and there is something you can do. We believe that in every interpersonal interaction each player shares equal responsibility for the communication, how it's given and how it's received. You are 100 per cent responsible for how you choose to communicate and react, and the other person is 100 per cent responsible for how they choose to communicate and react.

We want to encourage you to focus on getting clear about your end, despite any less-than-desirable communication from the other person. This includes interpreting another's communication, even the worst of it, in a way that works for you, leaves you intact and possibly even opens up an opportunity for personal growth.

Case study: letting go of blame

We once worked with a client who was reported to her department head by a team member for failing to run regular meetings for a group of managers, despite never having been given the accountability to run such meetings. We discovered the team member who made the report was intimidated by the department head, had performed poorly of late, felt insecure in his own position and wanted to deflect attention away from his own lack of effectiveness. Our client's first response was to get defensive; she verbally abused her team member in return for his unjustified complaints.

After we worked with our client for a number of weeks, she changed her tactics, and instead of trying to justify her current position and ensure blame was assigned appropriately, she chose to let go of her focus on the manipulative team member, and focus instead on improving herself. She chose to see the situation as an opportunity to develop her leadership skills, and ultimately took on tasks beyond her current role, taking full responsibility for the management meetings. Six months later she was promoted, while the questionable team member was let go.

Avoid the popularity stakes

One of the critical mistakes made by leaders, managers and supervisors is that they prioritise being popular (or becoming popular) with the members of their team ahead of being effective leaders, and in doing so, open themselves up to exploitation by the emotional manipulators.

Have you ever worked for a manager who seems to step over the manager-employee boundary in order to be liked by everyone? Who buys into the office chit-chat and gossip and aims to be a little too chummy with their team? This is just one of the things that is guaranteed to create problems, eventually.

One problem is that there's an inherent power imbalance in these relationships, which creates conflict and tension. The very nature of being a manager means that, at some point you'll be required to manage the performance of team members, and the chummy relationship will get in the way of effective performance conversations. The other problem with this approach is that it makes it easier for the emotional manipulators to get what they want: it gives them a way of exploiting your position of power for their interests. Trying to be popular is usually pretty obvious behaviour, and the bluffers will buddy up with you by saying the right things to make you feel good about yourself. The problem is that they will then use their friendly relationship with you to their advantage, to get away with things that you wouldn't normally allow around the office.

Trying to be popular with the emotional manipulators is like showing your hand to an opponent in a poker game and then asking for advice on how to win—they will suck you in by helping you win a small bet to start with, but will use the knowledge against you when the big pile of chips is on the table.

Rather than open yourself up to compromising situations by trying to be one of the team, it's important that you seek other strategies to connect in meaningful ways.

Here are some ideas to help you with this:

- Leave the gossip for the gossipers, and champion transparent communication.

- Satisfy your close buddy needs by connecting with colleagues at the same managerial level.

- Maintain professional, fair and equitable relationships with all team members (people will connect with those they respect).

- Network with other professionals and managers outside work.

- Engage in external coaching or mentoring relationships for your own professional development.

It's only natural as a manager to seek connection with your staff as close friends, and to be seen as popular among them, and we're not saying that you can't be friendly with your team. What we are saying is that it's important to be detached from the need for close attention from your staff. Set clear boundaries that keep roles clearly delineated, not only to manage all relationships fairly, but also to avoid exploitation by the bluffers who are ready to pounce on needy managers. When it comes to building your team, prioritise what works ahead of what feels good.

Engagement versus popularity

Throughout this book we have talked about the importance of engaging with your team, so this talk about not prioritising popularity may seem like a contradiction. There is a big difference between popularity and engagement. The difference relates to the drivers of these approaches. If the focus and concern is on yourself, then you will pursue popularity; if the focus is on others, then you will pursue engagement. Aim for engagement over popularity—it gets much more stuff done and gives far less ammunition to the emotional snipers out there.

Understanding intimidation and shaming

The first port of call here is to set your mind on one of our favourite mantras (already mentioned in chapter 7): 'It's not all about you'. The phrase reminds us that when people use intimidation and shame, it tells you more about what's going on in their worlds than about what you've done (although it may not feel this way), even when what they say is directly about you.

If the perpetrator of the aggressive, bullying behaviour is the psychopathic type, it's useful to remember that they are wired differently, and it's critical not to get caught up in asking why they may be doing this, or in trying to fix their behaviour. Instead, focus on how you can close down the situation.

Remember that the more common, non-psychopathic manipulator doesn't directly intend to hurt—although they do intend to get their way—but their behaviour is most likely founded on insecurity. For this kind of bluffer, you can remind yourself that such intimidation tactics are an indicator that they're suffering themselves. Much of the difficult behaviour, which can manifest as bullying, is protection against a deeper fear of not being good enough. The tough part for you is that they may not even be conscious of their deep-rooted insecurity, so it won't help to point it out to them. This is not about making excuses for their behaviour, but about seeing the reasons for it, and we know that understanding can help you take things less personally and respond more effectively.

Case study: the compassionate bully

We worked closely for a number of years with an executive-level leader who came across as a bully to many who knew him in the organisation. His behaviour justified the label of 'bully' because he would ask people to do unreasonable tasks and then berate them in front of their colleagues for not completing the tasks properly.

We got to understand, from working closely with him, that he was deeply caring about all the people in his workforce (he just didn't have a very good way of showing it). In fact, worrying about their job security kept him awake at night! The problem was, his behaviour was filtered through a self-image that included some killer doubts regarding his ability to lead people (the origins of which came from abusive childhood experiences), and in a protective,

(continued)

Case study: the compassionate bully *(cont'd)*

albeit unintentional, attempt to hide his insecurities from staff, he projected those negative self-feelings onto others. The issue was that he created a self-justifying system of fear, intimidation and subsequent poor performance; that is, he was overly hard on people, pushed them around and pushed people's buttons, stimulating their insecurities, so that they often avoided him—and some of their critical work tasks—which led to reduced productivity and justified his attacks on their performance.

The good-news ending to this story is that this man changed; he totally transformed himself and his business along with him. In the process, he got to see that the biggest thing holding him back was a deep personal fear connected to the stuff he experienced as a child. He learned to let go of that stuff and see that it no longer had to define him.

His personal transformation took quite a while, probably more than two years, and over that time we also had to work with the people around him to develop some practical strategies for dealing with his imposing behaviour.

So you can see that bullying behaviour can be a result of other deeper issues. Once you've got an awareness that there can be a bigger context outside of the behaviour you're seeing, it's useful to focus on the following tips for dealing with bullying behaviour.

Tips for dealing with bullying behaviour

Here are our top tips for understanding and dealing with bullying.

* *Pay attention to the incongruence.* If the behaviour doesn't match the situation (that is, it's overly reactive, critical or negative), acknowledge that there's possibly something else going on for the person, at a personal level, that probably has nothing to do with the current issue confronting you, and certainly nothing to do with you personally.

- *See past the mask.* If the bully in question is not likely to be a psychopath (refer to the section at the beginning of the chapter on how to spot a psychopath), work hard to find the possibilities for goodness and potential for growth in that person. Don't hesitate to express these thoughts clearly and frequently—tell them and others around them the possibilities you see. If you don't see what's possible for them, they won't see possibility in themselves.

- *Shore up your own resources.* Work on building your own confidence through personal and professional development, get extra leadership and tough-stuff communication training, engage a coach or a mentor, avoid going into interactions with the bluff stuff when you're overwhelmed with stressors, and seek support from a senior leader in your workplace if you're not feeling up to the task.

- *Create opportunities within the chaos.* When we get strong opposition, reaction or negative feedback from others, it's confronting and can cause us to go into a tailspin of negative self-meaning-making. Becoming aware that you've been manipulated can leave you feeling pretty lousy. But it's critical that, no matter what the manipulator says or does, you remind yourself that the miserable feelings you may experience result from a projection of their baggage, not a reflection of yours. Set your mind to grow from the adversity and always ask yourself, 'What can I learn from this experience?'

- *If you are really brave, summon the courage to give them honest feedback.* Because they are intimidating and manipulative, bullies rarely receive honest feedback from their peers or even from superiors. It may take some sensitivity to timing, context and best delivery method, but find a way to give them straight stuff. If they have any self-respect, they will respond more positively and, ultimately, will respect you more as a result.

Dealing with passive–aggressive behaviours

Emotional manipulators can be masters of passive–aggressive behaviours. Passive–aggressive behaving and communicating is characterised by someone who says 'yes' to your face but 'no' to your back. They appear compliant, but they will undermine a situation when they are removed from the conversation with you. The passive–aggressive is someone who, when asked to finish off the quarterly peer reviews, says 'no worries', but then spends the week complaining to everyone else in the team about the waste of their valuable time, and then doesn't deliver to deadline. They feel no sense of accountability, and that makes you look bad in front of your boss. Herein lies the core of their subversive aggression: 'Don't try to tell me what to do. I'll find a way to make you pay for it!'

Passive–aggressive behaviour can be difficult to manage because of the mixed messages being sent. This behaviour is not overt: it's covert, and it can easily turn into a 'he said, she said' mess, creating the type of confusion that allows the passive–aggressive bluffer to further avoid responsibility.

When you're faced with passive–aggressive behaviour, the best thing you can do is adopt some simple strategies around accountability:

- *Clarify your expectations with all members of your team.* Check and recheck that all your requests have been fully understood. It's easy for someone to justify poor behavioural integrity if your communication has been lacking.

- *Ensure agreement on the context and purpose of a request.* At the heart of all accountability is an agreement. It's pretty hard to tell people what to do and expect a result if you don't get their permission first. An example is the client who copped the blame for not running management meetings. Instead of trying to justify her lack of responsibility she could have sought, and documented, input and agreement from the team of managers with regard to why and for what objectives they would hold regular meetings, so that everyone shared accountability for making those meetings happen.

- *Create a paper trail of the expectations.* Publicly post expectations, where appropriate, and follow up any requests with an email to confirm what has been requested.

- *Get commitment to specific dates and times for completion.* Vague deadlines give the bluffers an excuse to procrastinate.

- *Maintain your own integrity about getting stuff done.* Do as you say and you'll stand tall in the tough-stuff conversations with those who don't do as they say.

- *Give straight feedback about the incongruence between words and actions.* Outline to others the difference between what they have said and what they have done. For instance, 'I recall you said you'd be able to get the peer reviews finished this week, and yet they haven't been done. I'm wondering what is happening here?' It's important to be inquisitive rather than accusatory in these conversations, as people can become defensive, but be courageous and tell it how it is.

Strategies for dealing with the bluff stuff

No matter which type of bluffer you're confronted with, it can be helpful to have some overarching strategies, and we hope to leave you with some here.

- *Move difficult conversations into context before dealing with the content.* When you're having bluff-stuff conversations, it can be very easy to find yourself getting stuck in the picky details of the situation. Content-based discussions require rationality, and in many emotionally charged situations rationality has left the building. Focusing on big-picture context issues first can help people come down from the emotional overwhelm. When they are more rational, they will be open to hearing the content details. For example, if you are trying to resolve a conflict over the minor errors in a proposal, begin by moving beyond the analysis of what actually happened, and focus on why it may have happened and why polished proposals are important to the business's bottom line.

- *Identify the bluffers.* Do your due diligence on the behaviours of different kinds of manipulators so that you can focus on the most effective responses for each of them. It's not within most managers' scope to diagnose psychopathy, nor any other personality disorder, but it is important to have some idea of what you may be dealing with. If you're not dealing with a psychopath, you will still have to take on a massive challenge to your patience and compassion to deal with emotional manipulation in the workplace.

■ *Take responsibility for your role in reinforcing the behaviours.* Be aware of how you contribute to the situation, and possibly make it easier for the bluffers to continue their manipulative ways. Vying for the most-popular-around-the-office title is not going to help because it will lay you open to manipulation. Be focused on being a manager, not a mate.

■ *Depersonalise the bullying and get past the surface behaviours.* For the non-psychopathic bully, remember there's a difficult personal story under there somewhere. Aggressive behaviour is most likely a projection onto you and others of the suffering going on inside. That's not to give them excuses for being a bully: it's about getting to a deeper level of connection, where it's much more possible to understand and change their dysfunctional behaviour.

■ *Create a culture of accountability.* Be accountable and demand accountability in return. Accountability in the workplace functions only if its leaders are pillars of integrity. When you do as you say, the manipulator can't exploit your lack of integrity as a weakness. Furthermore, by following the rules of the accountability game—clarity, agreement, commitment and follow-up—you'll close the door on the bluffer's excuse machine. And remember, you can still do accountability with compassion. Ultimately, keeping others on task for something that will be good for them is a form of compassion. It's similar to a situation where a true friend keeps you accountable to a healthy diet—and doesn't let you eat junk food—when they know you're trying to improve your health.

■ *Focus on solutions rather than problems.* We know that the reason we have tough-stuff conversations at all is because something is not working, but often the problems take up most of our attention. The bluffers are good at keeping the personal, emotional problems front and centre. A far more constructive conversation, one that goes right past all the emotional manipulation, is where you spend most of the time defining solutions and helping people to identify how they can resolve problems.

Conclusion

The world's most famous line about poker, 'You gotta know when to hold 'em, and know when to fold 'em' is also true when it comes to dealing with the different types of bluffers. It means you have to hold onto hope and put in an effort when dealing with a non-psychopathic bluffer, but fold up the table and do whatever you can to disengage from the true psychopathic bluffer.

In the absence of certainty about the personality you are dealing with in a workplace bluff-stuff conversation, the best you can do is make yourself part of the solution rather than part of the problem. None of this will be easy. This is as much about mindset as it is about a set of behavioural tools, and it will require you to prioritise what works ahead of what you may want. It means putting in extra time and energy to understand some of the complexities of human beings at work, and changing some of your own behaviours.

Darren's insights

I hear coaching clients say 'and then she turns on the waterworks when she doesn't get her way', as though this is step four in a five-step plan. Sometimes I think my clients believe their staff members must have sat there before the meeting thinking to themselves, 'When we reach the 27-minute mark I'm going to burst into tears'. If this were the case, what a privilege it must have been to have Academy Award-winning actor Meryl Streep working for them!

Too often we view emotional manipulation as Machiavellian behaviour, but my experience shows that's not always the case. Sure, there are some people in the workplace whose behaviour is incomprehensible. It seems reprehensible. But in most cases, emotional manipulation is used for one simple reason: it works!

People use emotional manipulation because it works and, more importantly, because you made it work for them. Repetition of this behaviour is simply based on cause and effect.

Ultimately, you get to decide whether you take someone's bluff or call it.

Alison's insights

There is always function in dysfunction. The behaviours we see as emotional manipulation in the workplace are often underpinned by hurt, fear and shame. While you may never have the opportunity to find out what is behind the behaviour, having this recognition in the back of your mind can be a useful way of finding some level of compassion towards others (as hard as that may be at times).

When it comes to dealing with emotional manipulation, passive–aggressiveness, bullying or intimidation within the workplace, it's important to be aware of your capacity to cope and look after yourself. Your ability to cope with situations changes all the time depending on what else is going on in your life. Being able to cope with someone else's behaviour with confidence and a sense of certainty within yourself requires a steady sense of health and wellbeing. Listen to your body and take positive action towards things that are important to you. Increasing your body intelligence by tuning in to how your body reacts to your experiences is key to dealing with the bluff stuff.

Sean's insights

For most of my life I have had a default tendency to assume people have the best intentions and that there is always more in someone than we can currently see, even if what we see looks pretty darn ugly. Then I took Bob Hare's forensic psychology class during my undergraduate degree, and I learned that I could be wrong in my rosy assumptions when it came to psychopaths.

I didn't give up my general positive regard for people, but I did learn a thing or two about approaching the bluffers differently. I believe the trick in dealing with the bluff stuff is to apply an obsessive level of discernment to understanding what may be driving someone's dysfunctional behaviour. Continue to seek the best in people, but be prepared to deal with the worst. When you get this one right, you can change organisations and transform cultures.

Chapter summary

- In every bluff-stuff situation, begin with the recognition that it's not all about you. Emotional manipulation comes either from a dysfunctional brain (in the case of the psychopath) or from a place of hurt, pain and fear (in the case of the damaged survivor). That's their stuff, not yours.

- Be responsible for your contribution to any interaction, even if the blame for poor outcomes belongs to someone else.

- In the face of snakes in suits or skirts (psychopathic bluffers), an essential strategy is to minimise their impact. Failing that, remove yourself from the connection, wherever possible. If removal is impossible, focus on dealing with day-to-day tasks rather than being dragged into emotional content by these manipulators.

- Responding effectively to intimidating or bullying behaviour demands that you don't take it personally: see past the negative stuff they're projecting and find the courage to ask for help if you feel depleted.

- Dealing with the bluff stuff is also about clarifying expectations, keeping others accountable and concentrating on context over content.

- In the face of passive–aggressive behaviour, set clear parameters about accountabilities and challenge the perpetrator about their behaviours directly and expediently when they step outside the boundaries.

- If someone in the workplace is just downright aggressive, pull back from the content battles, especially if the person is wound up. Focus on the context instead.

- As a person of influence, your stuff is all about the actions you take. Build confidence from action and focus on behaviour-based solutions to strengthen yourself, your team and the organisation.

PERFORMING
UNDER PRESSURE
is more about
PRACTICE
THAN
PERFECTION.

11

DEALING WITH THE OFF-THE-CUFF STUFF

Building skills to handle immediate crises

You may have heard that people show their true colours when they are under pressure. In psychology–speak, we say that the *default response*, the most well-worn brain pattern, is the one that shows up when the proverbial stuff hits the fan. The question is: how effective is your default response inside the pressure cooker of sudden, unexpected tough stuff in your workplace? Do you manage this off-the-cuff stuff well and produce positive outcomes during a crisis? Or is that the very moment that things tend to fall apart?

A crisis presents as a particular type of tough stuff, most often characterised by unexpectedness, uncertainty, a threat to important goals or a change to demands.

We believe there are three key areas to address in effectively dealing with a crisis. They are:

- how you turn up to a crisis situation
- how you deal with the aftermath
- how you prepare for future crisis events.

In this chapter we will unpack these points and discuss how you can apply them to the off-the-cuff stuff in your workplace.

Turning up to a crisis situation

Successfully dealing with tough stuff that occurs in the moment rarely requires just a reactive response. Most, if not all, leaders who handle the off-the-cuff stuff well share a common characteristic: they proactively arm themselves with the right way of thinking and never substitute genetics for hard work.

Crucial to achieving desired outcomes in the off-the-cuff stuff is exercising a possibility mindset; that is, challenging yourself to see what is possible when the odds are stacked against you.

Seeing possibility creates freedom

If you don't see possibilities, the likelihood of achieving success drops dramatically. Imagine your sales team has reached only 50 per cent of its target with two months to go until the end of the financial year, and the result could mean the business will be restructured, and jobs lost. Achieving budget may seem highly improbable, but if you and your team buy into that improbability, you will guarantee failure. If you've decided that something is not possible before you try to achieve the goal, the brain will shut down motivation and effort faster than you can blink an eye. Why? Because it's a simple survival mechanism: the conservation of energy. In ancient times there were many more occurrences of famine than feast, and as a result human beings became expert in conserving energy.

Not wasting energy can be important for survival and for being effective at work, but our energy shut-down mechanisms often kick in when we don't need them. To deal effectively with a crisis—such as being significantly behind budget at a turning point in the business—takes energy, creativity and openness to what's possible so that we keep stimulating the brain to find new and more effective courses of action.

Case study: don't let failure become a self-fulfilling prophecy

We worked with an automotive company coming out of the global financial crisis of 2008–09. When it was threatened with the closure of its foreign offices, we saw a group of leaders with pessimistic outlooks on growth for the next few years. There were a lot of (justifiable) rumours that the company might not exist past the second quarter of that year. Based on past events, projected targets and increasing costs, business failure was a stark reality. But if the leaders in the company stuck to a probability mindset and didn't see ambitious stretch goals as possible to achieve, they were likely to fulfil their low expectations.

When we are discouraged, we simply don't do the things that make a difference, and failure becomes a self-fulfilling prophecy. What the leaders in that company did was focus on a 'possibility ahead of probability' mindset, ultimately innovating and acting their way out of a dire situation.

If you are to have any hope of getting through a crisis powerfully, you have to be able to imagine possibilities for solving it.

Practised preparedness versus birthday gift

You may be capable of conjuring up the possible solutions to a crisis in your head, but you could still feel concerned that you lack the natural talent for executing those solutions. People generally put crisis response capability in the trait category, thinking of it as something you are either good at or not, or that it is part of your genetic make-up. 'Gee, Sam is fantastic under pressure. Cool head—she's just that kind of gal'. Maybe you think of it as a special leadership gene—the one that maybe you missed out on and only the people from planet fabulous are lucky enough to receive at birth. However, being effective in a crisis is not a gift from birth; it's a preparedness practised throughout life.

We've seen too many examples of managers who have transformed their crisis leadership skills from implosive to impressive to buy into the genetics argument.

In her book, *Mindset: The new psychology of success*, Stanford researcher on motivation, personality and development Carol Dweck draws a distinction between a fixed versus a growth mindset. In a fixed mindset, you believe your capabilities are more or less determined by birth and don't leave a lot of room for improvement. In a growth mindset, you believe your capabilities are flexible and can be improved significantly with time and effort. When you believe your ability to deal with the off-the-cuff stuff is fixed—something you have or don't have—rather than something you can learn, and you combine that with not feeling too good about your current capability, you may find yourself trying to avoid the prickly predicaments or jumping in awkwardly and stuffing things up even more.

But in crisis situations, the application of a growth mindset works and awesome responses can result. There's an opportunity to develop the skills of effective crisis response, and the way to start is to foster the growth mindset. So, for example, maybe you've lost your cool with a direct report during a high-pressure time in the business—for being late for a critical meeting, not following up with a key customer or making a simple error in a crucial sales document. Reflect on how you handled the situation: did your self-talk include comments such as, 'I've got to put more practice into handling pressure and I could benefit from some work on that', or was it more like, 'I've never been good under pressure, and there's not much I can do about it anyway'? If your response was more like the second statement, it's time to challenge your mindset and see that growth is possible.

Growth mindset, however, is not simply a thing you can tap into on a whim, especially under extreme pressure. If you're not well practised in the growth mindset, the more instinctual parts of your brain can take over. Like the emotional hijacking that occurs with rising anger (see chapter 6), under pressure your reptilian brain can hijack your problem-solving mechanisms. Crisis situations tend to stimulate the fight-or-flight response, the instinctual survival response designed to help you respond to physically harmful threats. In this response, the brain perceives a circumstance as threatening and triggers the release of hormones adrenaline and noradrenaline, which prepare the body for violent muscular action so you're ready to stay and fight the threat or run quickly from it.

When businesses are going through a crisis (perhaps a major budget cut or restructure), employees in fight-or-flight mode tend to let the small stuff slip, such as accountability for daily tasks. However, managers who are good during a crisis at motivating their staff to stay accountable for things such as timely meeting attendance or good customer service have learned how to keep their own survival emotions in check and how to respond well to the pressure overload. These managers respond to crises by interpreting perceived threats as manageable, and by using calming strategies such as deep breathing, time-outs and non-judgemental perspective-taking so that they aren't hijacked by their limbic system in the first place.

If you aren't quite there on the cool-headed approach, the way to improve is, first, to believe it is possible: see your capability as adaptable, not fixed; and, second, to practise identifying the strong survival emotions for what they are (overreactions to perceived threats). Practise thinking through your reactions to these emotions rather than responding automatically so that you can select an effective solution to the circumstances.

Case study: MD's worst nightmare

Sandy, a newly appointed managing director of a medium-sized organisation, stepped into a time bomb of a situation. Within two months of starting, Sandy was confronted first with an employee grievance in which the staff member was involved in a public altercation with his direct boss, and then with a situation where an executive team member was implicated in sexual indiscretions with two other members of staff. At the same time Sandy was dealing with a merger that was threatening a major overhaul of the organisational structure.

These problems were causing significant unrest throughout the workforce, and some of the company's best talent was threatening to walk out the door because they believed the workplace culture had no foundation of integrity. The business was losing money amid the interpersonal crises.

Sandy was overwhelmed by her own emotional responses. At first she struggled to see much possibility in the situation and wasn't sure if she was the right person to fix the problems. She initially reacted by withdrawing, avoiding the explosive issues she faced and hoping that they might go away. However, her avoidance only made matters worse: staff saw her as lacking authority and confidence, suggesting she was one of the reasons the culture was a mess and the business was failing.

Sandy feared failing at her new role and being held responsible for the downfall of a company in the midst of a hurricane of serious staff issues, a situation she had inherited. Sandy did lack some confidence, understandably, but with support, coaching and plenty of practice at seeing herself, her emotions and the solutions differently, she was able to gain control.

Sandy developed a task-oriented mindset: she saw that it wasn't about finding people to blame, but finding actions to take that would solve the problems in the company. She transformed her thinking to see the situation as a challenge, rather than as a threat, and as an opportunity for her to grow as a leader and make a difference to a faltering company. Her primary focus became execution of key actions to deal with the priorities, such as conducting a cultural audit so that she could target the problem areas, creating an open and honest forum of communication with her leadership team, and providing skills training for her staff to help them manage the crisis and keep them engaged in their roles. She also chose to let go of her desire to control the uncontrollables, such as the financial losses from the first half of the year, the exit of a number of key investors and her feelings of guilt about not doing enough, quickly enough, to sort out the problem.

Two years later, the company had doubled its revenue targets and was acknowledged in the industry as a top-100 employer of choice.

We will revisit some of the clever things that Sandy achieved in handling her situation, but before we do let's shift our focus to the second key area of handling the off-the-cuff stuff: how you can deal with what happens after the incident.

Dealing with the aftermath

The emergency situation has passed, and the fight-or-flight response has diminished. Although there is often some residue from the experience, there is a greater sense of calm. Being able to assess the fallout and pick up the pieces is an important step in dealing with these tough situations. There are two matters to address when dealing with the aftermath of a crisis: first, recognising the importance of resolving the heightened emotions that were experienced during the situation; and second, exploring and making meaning from the experience.

Resolve emotions

If you've conquered the peak of the crisis, it's time to resolve emotions—and quickly. You must acknowledge and work through any emotional impacts of the crisis situation as soon as possible—that is, deal with the crises after the crisis.

Contradicting ourselves may seem like a poor tactic to convince you of the strength of our arguments, but in a crisis you have to be ready to manage contradiction and uncertainty. As quickly as you've tuned out the personality and relationship stuff in front of you, to ensure that the boardroom negotiation was effective or that serious injury was averted, you have to tune back in and work hard to resolve the emotional fallout with the different individuals involved. We can't emphasise this enough. People will tell you they're doing fine in the aftermath of a chaotic workplace storm, but they're often not great judges of, or therapists for, themselves and the state of their emotions.

We have only to look at the horrific long-term effects of unaddressed post-traumatic stress disorder (PTSD) among survivors of Vietnam and other wars to realise that the suppression of emotional trauma is not effective beyond more than a few minutes—hours at most. In a more recent example, mental health researchers Joseph Boscarino, Richard Adams and Charles Figley showed that people who received worksite crisis interventions offered by their employers after the terrorist attacks on the World Trade Center in New York in 2001 experienced benefits across a spectrum of outcomes—compared with individuals who didn't get any help—including reduced risk of binge drinking, alcohol dependence, PTSD symptoms, major depression and anxiety.

Being a victim of terrorism is probably one of the most extreme forms of crisis: something not representative of what managers face in the workplace. Nonetheless, the process of acknowledging and working through people's emotions is critical. You're not expected to be anyone's psychotherapist, but what you can do as a manager is follow a number of useful steps:

- *Empathise.* Try to put yourself in other people's shoes to imagine what it might feel like for them and communicate your empathy to those people.

- *Acknowledge publicly that whatever anyone feels is normal.* The entire range of emotions in response to a crisis is normal: there is no right or wrong way to feel at any time.

- *Coach people to get to a place of acceptance about what they have been feeling.* This is more effective than reinforcing that they block out their emotions.

In the case of significant crises, where individuals (including yourself) have had difficult emotional responses, help people to get professional support, whether it's through an internal employee assistance program or external consultants.

Manage meaning

Once the peak of the crisis has passed, work with your team to make healthy meaning out of *why* the crisis happened and how you will grow from it. Often, people can think they have got past a crisis and have put it behind them, only to relive the trauma of it all over again when it pops back into memory a few months, and sometimes years, later In the workplace, if there have been interpersonal conflicts during the crisis, as there were in Sandy's organisation in the case study, while immediate tensions may have diminished once the crisis settled down, unresolved tensions can be reignited in a future crisis.

The effective way to put a crisis behind you is to create positive, adaptive associations to the experience. This is not an easy process. It takes creativity and fortitude. But it gives you power and real strength to move on and respond effectively to future crises. You need to come up with positive reasons for *why* it all happened. For example, 'Although it was tough, that restructure was probably needed to get us thinking about how we can be more efficient with our time management', or 'We didn't really need to lose three of our major sponsors to acknowledge that our strategy had to change, but I believe that crisis was a turning point for us. Without it, we probably would not have come up with these innovative ideas for growth'.

There may always be some tough emotions for people when they reflect on a crisis, but making positive meaning of the experience is the difference between bouncing back from it and stagnating for the rest of your career.

Preparing for future crisis events

We talked earlier about possibility versus probability. Sandy's situation, described in the case study, shows it is also essential to prioritise the actions that deliver on the possibility, rather than getting caught up in the negative results going on around you. Focusing on negative outcomes is like getting caught up in the gawk phenomenon on a highway, where drivers stare at a car wreck rather than focusing on good driving to get past it, which creates more traffic jams and accidents. Focusing instead on the conditions that caused the crash is how you can avoid becoming part of the pile up.

Prioritise: control the controllables

In a future crisis, you have to focus on actions, but not just any actions. The things that matter most in a crisis are the actions that will make a difference and that are in your immediate control, not the outcomes going on around you that you can't control. We often use an expression with our high-performance clients that is relevant for those having to sort out a tough situation under extreme pressure: 'fail going 100 per cent'. This means being okay with the unavoidable failures as long as you're doing everything you can to achieve the outcomes over which you do have control. When people get caught up in the failures that they can't control anyway, it just reduces the precious few resources they have for tackling the priority actions in a crisis.

Focus on the future first

If you were in the situation of being behind in your budget targets late in the year, there's no point in focusing on what did or didn't happen for the first three financial quarters, which are now in the past. There's also no point in complaining to your team about how the global economic situation or current consumer attitudes have been destroying your sales numbers. The priority has to be what action you and your team can take in the final months of the year—such as following up on stagnating customers already in the sales pipeline, prioritising quick-turnaround lead generation and finding business in unexpected markets—to make budget. By all means take lessons from the environment that caused the previous poor results, but keep your focus on the most important outcomes or priorities.

Expert in dealing with crises, retired US general Russel L. Honoré (the former commander of Joint Task Force Katrina), who oversaw the military relief efforts after the devastating hurricanes of 2005 in the Gulf Coast, reminds us of the importance of prioritising critical action: 'Try to quickly assess the number-one priority...if the number-one priority is to save lives and people understand that, then that will trump a lot of the other conversations or good ideas that come up'.

Less planning, more practising

Jonathan Clark and Mark Harman, experts on crisis management, remind us that an effective crisis management plan is founded on two distinct principles:

- You can't plan for every possible crisis that might occur.

- Practising or rehearsing your response to potential crises can make all the difference.

Studies of crisis management will remind you that anticipating and preparing for crises using scenario or contingency planning is essential for an effective response. However, recent research has revealed that crisis planning may not have any significant association with the effectiveness of crisis management, and in some cases a high level of crisis planning could get in the way of implementing decisions and create rigidity that blocks a team's effectiveness in getting things done.

Planning for a workplace crisis on its own can be like planning to run a marathon from the comfort of your couch without ever going for a run. The planning may even give you some (false) confidence, but no matter how well you plan the run, you won't achieve any gains in your physical fitness. Planning for crises could be setting you up for disaster if you don't have a way of rehearsing the crisis response. Planning is not enough and is sometimes downright counterproductive because it can paralyse effective action. It makes more sense to make crisis mindsets and behaviours a regular part of your routine.

A good mate of ours, founder of the Global Thought Leaders movement and guru on professional speaking Matt Church, calls this process 'practised spontaneity'. Form effective habits through regular practice that you can then draw on spontaneously when you need them.

Surveys tell us that the greatest fear among people in the modern world is speaking in public. Fight or flight isn't much use when you step up onto a stage and try to deliver a compelling message to a large, expectant audience. How smooth and engaging is your CEO's presentation at the annual conference? Have you ever watched a comedian shoot from the hip, spontaneously engaging with different audience members? If the person fails in either of these situations, the result can be utter humiliation. What professional speakers and comedians (and the rare CEO) do is practise what they want to say and how to say it in so many different ways and in so many different sequences that on the day they can be spontaneous in terms of when and how they deliver their practised material, drawing the right response for different audiences at the right time without missing a beat. What they are saying may look made up at the time, but the content is incredibly well rehearsed—it is the method and moment of delivery in context that is the spontaneous part.

Going back to our case study of Sandy, the approach she decided to work on was developing skills that would serve her and the team at all times, in crisis or in calm. Sandy focused on being open and authentic in her feedback to all her staff (and reinforced them to do the same with each other). She initiated the tough conversations when the issues were still small, before they could blow up into big problems, and she constantly checked in with key members of her staff to get an emotional barometer of the team, so that she could provide coaching and other resources to help manage and minimise the escalation of interpersonal tension. Learning and practising the techniques for effective management were going to be the best tools for Sandy to manage any future crises that might arise.

Choose your daily behaviours carefully—if you are complacent and practise mediocrity when things are easy, you can only expect to get mediocrity when things get tougher.

Conclusion

As much as you may plan for it, a crisis is pretty much defined as a situation that you can't be totally prepared for. A crisis is different from a simple failure in that it demands significant and immediate change, and you and your team will be stretched to adapt effectively. What will make all the difference is if you practise the key mindsets and behaviours outlined in this chapter regularly, regardless of whether you're in crisis or not.

Remember, given that there is probably no perfect response for dealing with a crisis, if you are in constant action around the suggested strategies, you will be ahead of 99 per cent of people in responding to crises.

Darren's insights

I sometimes think the off-the-cuff stuff is where we can learn our most valuable lessons. In the moment it may be hard to be the student, but the lessons often come after the off-the-cuff stuff—providing you reflect on your own actions and have the courage to put them under the microscope.

Open yourself to diagnosis. Ask yourself forensic questions. Revisit the shifts you may have been able to make. This learning can drive future behaviours and help you achieve success. Don't beat yourself up if things don't go exactly to plan in the moment. Managing in a crisis rarely goes perfectly to script, but it is imperative you study your lines for the next time you have to play the part.

Alison's insights

During times of pressure leaders can get too hasty in taking the next step when, more often than not, a decision at work doesn't need to be made immediately. One of the key tools that I talk about with executive leaders is creating a decision gap—that is, allowing a gap between when you gather the information about a situation and when you make a decision about the next step. This gap may only be five minutes, it may be half an hour or it may be a day or two. But allowing yourself this space to step back can be the stimulus for effective problem solving.

Taking even a small breather in the midst of the chaos creates a space before jumping in and gives you the ability to sit back after the storm settles and feel confident that you made the best decision possible given the circumstances. This is the hallmark of a great leader.

Sean's insights

Because I have worked with a good number of professional athletes, I am asked all the time, 'How can I get better at performing under pressure?' People are seeking that magic bullet to make them invincible. My suggestion is that you have to put the work into developing you!

The best thing you can do to get good at managing the off-the-cuff stuff is to increase your daily habits around practising a resilient mindset. Make it a habit to think adaptively about results, failure and capability. First, choose to see that results are a measure of current skills and knowledge in the context of the immediate challenge that you can improve on — results are not a measure of unchangeable capability. Second, choose to see failure as feedback that you can use to improve your future responses rather than evidence that you are just not good enough and should probably give up.

Keep visualising the possibilities; keep getting into action and, in the words of British wartime prime minister Winston Churchill, 'Never, never, never give up'.

Chapter summary

- A crisis presents as a particular type of tough stuff, most often characterised by unexpectedness, uncertainty, a threat to important goals or a change to demands.

- Manage how you turn up to a crisis situation.

- See beyond current probabilities to what is possible, and exercise your growth mindset regularly.

- Being effective in a crisis situation is not a gift from birth but a preparedness practised throughout life.

- Develop strategies to deal with the aftermath of a crisis situation.

- Spend your energy on actions that will solve the problem, not on personalities or uncontrollable outcomes.

- Admit that there may be collateral damage in terms of thoughts and feelings, so you need to work hard to resolve the damage in functional ways once the peak crisis has passed.

- When you look back, make positive meaning of what happened and find the opportunities for growth.

- Prepare for and anticipate future crisis events.

- Accept that you will fail at some things, but do whatever you can to succeed at the things within your control.

There are times to
STRETCH
YOURSELF
and times to
RECHARGE;
success comes from
doing both.

12

DEALING WITH ENOUGH STUFF
Prioritising things that matter

As we reach the final chapter of this book, you may be reflecting on the journey of exploring, reframing and consolidating the behavioural and psychological approaches to dealing with the tough stuff. If you want to make the changes needed to map a clearer path in the tough-stuff conversations, you will need to achieve a certain level of discipline and commitment to deliver the results you want.

Think about the times when you operate at your best at work — when you have 20 tasks on the go but you are on top of all of them, and nothing is too much of a challenge. Well-known professor of psychology and management Mihaly Csikszentmihalyi describes this experience as 'flow'. If someone took a picture of you in this state, what would that image look like?

Now take the time to think about when you're operating at your worst at work: even the little things feel like they are an effort and deplete you of energy, and nothing goes according to plan. It's about here that you lock your keys in the car or leave your wallet at the café as you try to rush back to your work. How does this photo of you compare with the other one?

Now consider how differently you are equipped to deal with the tough stuff at work in these two different states. Your ability to have the tough conversations—and to keep calm, rational and clearheaded—when you're working at your best far outweighs your attempts at the tough conversations when you're operating at your worst. How we turn up to these conversations has a significant impact on the outcome, its success and your ability to put into place the practical strategies outlined in this book.

Your ability to deal with tough situations and engage in key conversations when they're needed is directly related to how well you're able to cope with pressure. Part of this is looking after yourself and knowing yourself well enough to be able to say, 'I've had enough. I need to revive, rejuvenate and restore to be able to tackle the next thing'. It's about knowing how to prioritise the things that matter in your life so that you have the energy to address the tough-stuff conversations successfully.

The mind is not always stronger than the body

Feeling driven to work harder and harder without giving ourselves a chance to rejuvenate is not sustainable, and at a certain point the body will step in and shut you down. We know that, as mere mortals, we need to acknowledge our emotional and physical limits. It's tough to admit to your humanity at times, but it's one of the most important things you can do to manage your energy levels and keep on top of your game. This takes a mindset shift.

In sport, for example, many athletes abide by the philosophy of more is better, but at some point the body will say that more is *not* better and will close up shop and send you messages of fatigue and low motivation to protect you from serious injury or illness. If you don't pay attention to your body's messages, you will harm your performance capacity and health for the long term. Sustainability is as much a concept for human beings as it is for the planet.

Perfectionists struggle with this one: 'You mean I can't strive to do more of the perfect program, more of the perfect project refinement?'. It can take extraordinary courage to admit to limits and vulnerability, but it may be the best thing you can do to keep yourself healthy and on track to achieving your personal and professional goals.

How much stress is enough stress?

Stress has been given a bad rap over the years. It's seen as something to avoid, but the truth is that we need a certain amount of stress to get moving, to drive action and to get things done. There's nothing like a looming deadline to put the pressure on and force us into action. Challenges give us purpose at work. If we were not given challenges, and all goals were easily attainable, there would be no reason to push ourselves beyond our perceived limits, and we wouldn't realise that we're actually capable of much more than we think.

When it comes to how much stress is enough, there's a tipping point. The performance-arousal curve illustrated in figure 12.1 (overleaf) shows that we need arousal, energy and a certain amount of stress to reach our peak performance. Around the top of the curve we're operating in our flow, when the balance between pressure and our ability to cope is fairly equal. There's a tipping point when performance starts to decrease as stress increases beyond the level we need to perform at our best. We start to let small things slip; we're no longer on top of it all. Then, as the pressure continues to increase, performance steadily declines until we reach the point where we're snapping at others and forgetting even straightforward things. (Putting the milk away in the oven can be a sign you've reached this point.)

Figure 12.1: the area of peak performance on the performance arousal curve

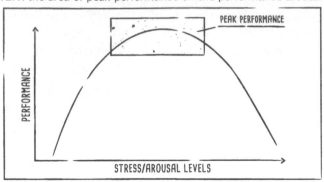

Knowing how much stress is enough stress is an individual thing. Some people have a higher stress threshold and it can seem like the greater the pressure, the more they excel. On the other hand, others may lose the plot at the pressure of having to attend a team meeting on time every week. The amount of stress we can take is also contextual — that is, it's related to what else is going on in our lives. Someone who can generally cope with a high level of stress but is dealing with caring for a sick parent while balancing the role of parenting and is perhaps also anxious about an impending restructure at work, for example, may have depleted resilience.

Knowing your tipping point is a crucial insight: know when you need to amplify the pressure and when you need to release the pressure. If you're working on the upside of the curve, the strategies to get into your area of peak performance will be different from those on the downside of the curve.

Insights about elite sport performance

Dr Sean Richardson has researched why elite athletes tip themselves past their peak performance point — past their limits — and end up in a heap on the way to achieving their biggest goals, regardless of the fact they have the knowledge to make better decisions about stressors and recovery.

212

One athlete, for example, was one of the best in the world in his sport: a three-time world champion, in the top three in the world for more than six years and a favourite to win gold at the next Olympics. Motivated by an intense desire to do more than ever before to ensure he sealed the gold at his home Olympics, he exceeded the limits, overtrained, got sick, was injured and finally missed out on competing in the Olympics altogether. The result was a long bout of depression and ultimate retirement from the sport. The costs of not acknowledging our limits can be enormous.

You need to consider the ABCs of human behaviour (see chapter 2) when it comes to managing your most valuable resource: you. Look at which antecedents to a behaviour might motivate you to make poor decisions about your health and wellbeing, particularly when the pressure is on to deliver on big targets.

At work we also need a mindset shift about the role of recovery in achieving peak performance, just as we would for peak performance in sport. This involves allowing ourselves time out and recognising mental, social, emotional and physical rejuvenation as being no less important for our work than the time and effort we put into getting our work done. The stress-recovery balance (the yin and yang of high performance) can't be ignored if we want to be able to perform at our peak when we need to.

Managing emotional overload

The problem is that we get reinforcement for overdoing it, and exhaustion has become a status symbol. There's a sense that we're not really having a go unless we're up to our eyes in work and burning the candle at both ends. The problem with societal approval of being overworked is twofold:

- Tiredness is detrimental to problem solving and innovation.
- People get caught up in being active instead of being productive.

Long-term, sustainable performance requires a balanced approach. We need to top up our energy stores on a weekly, if not daily, basis. For leaders, it's critical to courageously model the behaviour that says, 'I have a limit', or 'I'm not able to do that right now', or simply 'I don't know, so I won't push it'.

The research reminds us that no-one is immune to significant personal setbacks. Recent studies suggest that 20 per cent of people in the Western world will face significant depression or anxiety, and that's probably an underestimate! Think about the people around you at work. More than two out of every 10 people will be touched by a major personal, emotional crisis: are you prepared to deal with that? How do you have a conversation about sensitive topics with people at your workplace? How can you be supportive without becoming someone's therapist? How do you manage your own emotional overload?

Ramp up and bounce back

There are times when we need to stretch ourselves to break free from complacency, and times when we need to focus on recharging. Do one more than the other for too long and your performance will suffer. In order to keep within your area of peak performance you need to know when you need to ramp up your energy levels and when you need to relieve the pressure.

Ramping up the pressure

Sometimes sitting in a comfort zone actually reduces productivity, and in order to become more productive, more efficient and more effective you need to find strategies to ramp up the pressure and move into your area of optimal performance. When this is the case, you're best served by bringing some discipline to challenging yourself.

- Regularly seek discomfort. If you've been in a comfort zone for more than a week, it's time to stretch yourself a bit. (Revisit the vulnerability section in chapter 1 for some extra tips.)

- Set your own challenge. (If the boss wants a job done in five days, get it to them earlier than expected.)

- Create friendly competition with someone and be accountable to each other.

- Take on additional projects or roles.

- Develop new systems or new ways of doing the work.

Consider other things that could work for you as challenges and support in ramping up your energy to get things done.

Getting smart about relieving pressure and bouncing back

There are other times when too much pressure actually means we're operating in a state that's beyond our optimal performance and we would benefit from being able to relieve the pressure.

The latest research in human physiology tells us that sleep and good nutrition often aren't enough to replenish your energy, particularly if you have multiple stressors in your life—mental, physical, emotional, social and situational. You need to match your recovery activities (anything that puts energy back in) with the type of stressor (anything that takes energy away) you're experiencing. Here are some examples.

- If the main source of stress is physical (caused by, for instance, lack of sleep or lots of travel), match it with an appropriate physical recovery. Try getting more sleep, eat more nutritiously, try massage or physical therapies to help the body recover, or do some light exercise such as a walking or bike riding.

- If the source of stress is emotional (such as anxiety caused by work or issues in your personal life), match it with appropriate emotional recovery. Consider meditation, talking to supportive friends or colleagues, or getting some counselling or psychotherapy sessions.

- If the source of stress is social (caused by things such as tough interactions with people at work or in your personal life, difficult relationships or general lack of fun), match it with appropriate social recovery. Think about attending social nights out—minus any heavy drinking—such as movies, dinners, relaxing and fun conversation, or light, enjoyable physical activity.

- If the source of stress is mental or cognitive (caused, for instance, by working intensely on a project that demands high-pressure decision making), match it with the appropriate mental recovery. Meditation, time out, giving yourself permission to let go of worries for a specified period, and enjoyable mental activities such as relaxed book-reading and mentally relaxing light physical exercise could work.

Tune into what's going on for you at a particular time, physically, emotionally and socially, and then match your strategy accordingly. Ask yourself what you need more of and what you need less of to help you to operate at your personal best.

Helpful tips for releasing the pressure

In addition to the strategies outlined earlier, here are a few others for releasing pressure and reigniting your energy in order to be able to address the tough stuff most effectively.

- *Create a decision gap.* Often, we feel that decisions need to be made then and there at work. Where possible, create a space between taking in the information and making a decision. This space may be only five minutes, it may be an hour, or it may be a day or so. The amount of time is not relevant—what matters is recognising that most decisions can be given some space.

- *Reconnect to the things that are important to you.* When our values are clear, decisions are easy. Our values also give us meaning and motivation to keep on task.

- *Have a place and people you can easily connect with at the workplace.* This will help you to vent, which can help give you perspective.

In addition, think of other things that work for you.

It's important to recognise where you're sitting on the performance arousal curve at any given time so that you can match your activities accordingly. Do this more often and you'll be better equipped to deal and cope with the tough stuff when it arises.

Celebrate your progress

It's easy to jump from one project to the next, from one change to the next, from one tough conversation to the next, without taking the time to stop and recognise the progress we've made. The word 'celebrate' comes from the Latin word *celebrare*, which means 'assemble to honour'. In our projects at work or at home, we often overlook the milestones. Taking the time to honour progress doesn't require a fanfare. Simply sitting back and seeing how far you've come and what you've achieved can be enough. Gathering your team and the people around you who have contributed to the progress and saying thank you is incredibly important.

You are the company you keep

We all have a choice about the people we share our day and valuable time with. Generally, there are two sorts of people in our lives: those who put out our fire and those who ignite our fire. The fire-fighters are quick to put out your flame: they're cynical about the possibility of success. But the fire-lighters in your life inspire. You know the ones: the people you walk away from simply buzzing; the people you can't wait to catch up with again. The first group will deplete you of resources, but the other will refuel you with energy and possibility. Life is too short to be living by other people's self-limiting beliefs.

Just as physical exercise can build our fitness, consistent mental exercise will build our inspiration and creative muscle. You can exercise your brain and keep company with some of the leading experts from around the world by:

- reading the top 10 business books and articles
- connecting with other forward-thinkers

- watching one of the many speakers who showcase online at TED Talks offering ideas worth spreading. Ken Robinson's talk on creativity and Benjamin Zander's talk about sparkly eyes are good places to start

- turning off the television and getting engrossed in a stimulating conversation with one of your fire-lighters.

Make smart choices about the company you keep and you'll see how ordinary people can achieve extraordinary things. Being able to approach key conversations from this place of inspiration and enquiry is a powerful tool in dealing with the tough stuff as it provides perspective and new ways of considering a given situation.

Develop the skill of courage

We all have times in our working lives when we become frustrated by a certain aspect of our job, and there are times when this one aspect changes our whole outlook on the job. But there's a clear difference between the people who get stuck at this point, dreading going to work each day in a job they hate, and those who use this experience to their advantage. Invariably, the difference between getting stuck or moving forward is courage.

Courage is the catalyst that moves us from inaction to action.

From a simply economic viewpoint, few businesses, organisations or teams have singled themselves out from their competitors without the presence of courageous decision making. The leaders in almost every field of endeavour have rarely taken the path of least resistance. While doubt, anxiety, worry and hesitation provide valuable checks for measuring our potential course of action, they should not provide the reason for inactivity.

Courage in the workplace is seldom a response to an emergency event and, when used well, is planned, well timed and logical. Engaging in a courageous act at work is mostly a deliberate decision that requires planning and good timing. Consider where you may be able to use and develop courage at work through deliberate action. Maybe it's through the courage to:

- deal with difficult behaviour
- deal with conflict
- own your mistakes
- address your point of view with a manager
- make a decision
- deal with poor performance
- treat others better than they have treated you.

Before thinking about planned courage as a time-consuming or effort-filled process, remember this: a lifetime of change can often be brought about by just a few seconds of courage.

Do the stuff you're great at and outsource the rest

The Gallup organisation, which researches human nature and behaviour around the world, conducted a study in various countries and interviewed successful leaders with the aim of identifying the common qualities that great leaders possessed. What the organisation found was that there was only one common factor among the vast array of successful leaders they interviewed: these leaders worked within their strengths; they did the things that they were brilliant at, and they outsourced the rest.

This sounds straightforward but, on closer inspection, the ability of a leader to be open and transparent about the things they are not great at—to admit that there are areas of the job that would be much better left to someone else—takes a massive amount of courage. There's a common perception that our leaders should be great at everything, but the humble and the authentic freely admit that they're not, and then set up strategies and teams around them to bridge the gaps.

To become a better leader, play to your strengths. Get clear about the things you excel at and find ways of doing these things more often. This is not to say that there won't be stuff that you have to do that's not among your strengths, but aim for imbalance: aim to be playing to your strengths more often than not.

Create great habits

Today's habits are tomorrow's achievements. The decisions and actions you take today shape your future. For example, if you set yourself the goal of running a marathon, you need to develop the habit of running. Whatever you do consistently and repetitively will be your outcome.

What are today's habits predicting about your tomorrow? Are you equipping yourself to be in a better position to tackle the tough stuff when it arises? Are you practising the strategies from this book? If you stumble or get slightly off track, reaffirm what the next step is and take it rather than giving up. If you miss a week of training in the lead-up to the marathon, rather than throw out the goal, commit to making your next week of training truly count. Strengthen your great habits through the following:

- Make choices around *why*.
- Be clear on the method — *how* am I going to do it?
- Get moving into action — *what* can I do today?

These three practices create habits that predict tomorrow's successes.

Conclusion

Inspiration and motivation are terrific things to have on your side, but without a process that allows them to work, they soon wane. In order to take our suggestions forward and put them into practice, remember that things built to last are assembled one step at a time, with purpose and deliberate action.

As you move forward and prioritise your attention, make sure you have the capacity to know when enough is enough.

Darren's insights

I have been fortunate in my personal life to overcome some debilitating and destructive patterns of behaviour that threatened not only to sap my potential, but also my very existence. While my list of regrets is long, I have learned to live with them, and now actually believe the ability to accept my past wrongs gives me the steel and drive for my current success.

Along the winding pathway I have had to embrace my weaknesses and challenge my own self-limiting beliefs. It is a humbling and by no means easy process. As individuals and leaders we need to accept current reality, then work out what is the best next step without necessarily drafting a five-year plan.

Alison's insights

Human beings have an incredible capacity to endure hardship and uncertainty. For example, statistics show 20 per cent of soldiers who come home from war experience post-traumatic stress disorder. What is surprising to me is that this number is not higher. The trauma experienced by the other 80 per cent is not any less horrific or dramatic, but there is something in their ability to cope that equips them to deal with this experience and stands them in good stead.

The difference is in harnessing resilience and prioritising what is truly important. While the workplace only occasionally resembles a war zone, our need to focus on what aids us to cope with life's pressures is equally important. Your capacity to deal with the tough stuff for years to come without causing stress and burnout relies upon it.

Sean's insights

Often the biggest barrier to good decision making is concern for what others think about you. To avoid being perceived as weak or soft, people will too often choose to suffer in silence and not take action to get themselves right. We have learned to prioritise ego demands—the desire to look good—over our physical needs.

Satisfy both ego and physical needs with a shift in mindset, learning to take pride in a discipline around recovery. Be a person who has the strength to admit that you are human, flawed and susceptible to weakness, but one who is also committed to doing whatever it takes to get your mind, body and spirit back into balance. Ask for help, get a mentor, open up to a supportive friend, find a great psychotherapist, find out how to change your nutritional choices and learn about all the different ways you can take better care of yourself.

Chapter summary

- We deal with the tough stuff better when we operate at our best. Get in tune with what helps you work at your best.

- Get the balance right. Operating at our peak performance sometimes involves increasing the pressure and other times relieving it. Have strategies for both.

- Develop the skill of courage.

- Create great habits to achieve tomorrow's success. Start putting strategies into action so you will be better equipped to deal with the tough stuff.

- Do the stuff you are great at and outsource the rest.

- Rather than being overwhelmed by all the things that you have to do or should do, make a decision about what you will do. What is the next best thing you can do?

- Exercise your most powerful muscle: your brain.

- Surround yourself with fire-lighters and reduce your time with fire-fighters.

Diversity in human beings
should be seen as
both a

WORTHY
CHALLENGE

and a

WONDERFUL
GIFT.

CONCLUSION

We genuinely appreciate your time and dedication to reading our offering on how you can make your own tough stuff that bit easier. There's no doubt in our minds that if you put into practice the concepts we've explored, you'll achieve better results in your tough conversations.

We know that avoiding the tough conversations doesn't make the situation go away, and often avoidance can actually mean that the situation becomes blown out of proportion. One of the reasons why people avoid dealing with the tough stuff is a concern about upsetting another person, or being upset by their reaction. Unfortunately, this approach doesn't allow either person the opportunity for greater connection and understanding.

Being an effective leader requires you to step up, address what's unsaid and look for strategies for moving forward. In your process of moving forward, don't forget the really important stuff though—it isn't results, and it isn't outcomes. It's the person right in front of you.

Mum was right ... again

Remember when the most powerful reinforcer that drove your life was a few carefully chosen words of wisdom from mum? *You're special. You're unique. You're the best little girl/boy in the whole world.* Those few words made you feel great, didn't they?

Well it seems that mum's words of wisdom were exactly that: words of a futurist, prophet and professor all rolled into one. In today's world of unlimited choice, success is found in establishing a niche or standing out from the crowd. In dealing with the tough stuff at work, we can actually make the choice to celebrate these things. The differences between the people you lead or manage should be seen as a gift, not as a bugbear. It's in those differences that outstanding and extraordinary success lies.

But all too often we reject the outstanding and extraordinary in favour of conformity and mediocrity. We tend to encourage work that's similar to what other people, teams, departments, businesses and even our competitors are doing. This mentality can also drive our leadership efforts—for example, managing in a way that treats everyone the same when each person is beautifully and extraordinarily unique. In doing this we move towards walking, talking, thinking and acting the same. It's safer, but it also gives pretty average results.

The push to conformity in organisations is not exclusive to individuals: it also applies to teams. But in a big organisation, the successful teams aren't the same–same teams—they're unique and they're celebrated for their individuality.

Think about it. You've never heard someone say, 'The HR team at ABC organisation has a great reputation: it's exactly the same as everyone else'. What we actually hear is, 'They are outstanding. They do things so differently over there'.

The most influential writers and bloggers in the world at this moment see what Mum saw all those years ago: uniqueness is actually a currency, and a very valuable one at present. Specialists are needed now more than ever before.

In dealing with the tough stuff at work, it's important to recognise and celebrate the points of uniqueness, and embrace the fact that each person in front of you is not an employee who needs to be treated in the same way, but rather, a magnificently unique individual who needs unique and individual engagement.

What sort of boss or colleague are you?

Happiness seems to be a much sought-after commodity in this day and age. More and more organisations are realising that individuals are seeking far more than just a pay packet. They want to be inspired, to be part of something worthwhile, and most importantly they are seeking to be treated like human beings.

Adventurer and speaker Dan Buettner's book *Thrive* explores the components that contribute to long-term happiness in pockets of communities around the world. Buettner has discovered that there are individuals and workplaces that have uncovered the secrets of combining work and happiness, ensuring they're not only surviving, but thriving into the future.

Buettner mentions a Gallup-Healthways poll which showed that having the right boss is the single biggest determinant of workplace satisfaction. So what sort of boss are you? How are you contributing to your organisation surviving or thriving?

What struck us most about Buettner's list of qualities of a thriving boss was that none of the qualities spoke about the boss who had the best roster, or the best strategic plan for the team, or always kept within budget. Every single quality of a thriving boss involved having strong human skills, such as being approachable, providing regular feedback, establishing clear requirements, practising good listening and earning trust. We believe this same list of qualities works for connecting with colleagues and for generating long-term relationships with clients. If you aim to be approachable, to listen genuinely and to build trust, then your clients will keep coming back. And any businesses whose clients love what they do are thriving.

So as you step forward into your work today—whether it's managing others, working with colleagues or connecting with clients—seek to focus on the following things:

- *Make someone's day better.* Acknowledge the initiative, the foresight, the hard work and the joy of others. There's nothing more reinforcing than praise and acknowledgement.

- *Be approachable (no, really).* Remove yourself from your phone, your computer and any distractions, and be available to discuss challenges and problems with the person in front of you.

- *Get out of the way.* Once you've set clear expectations, get out of the way and let others do their job. If you're working directly with clients, this means getting your own agenda out of the way and listening to what's going on for them.

Practise what you preach

Modelling the behaviours you want to see in others is an important step to being able to deal with tough situations. Teams reflect their leadership and this is never more evident than in dealing with tough situations at work. Have the courage to make the changes in yourself that you want to see in others. If you want individuals in your team to step up to the plate and use their initiative, make sure you're doing this in your own role.

Often what you *do* has a greater influence on others than what you *say*. Matching your actions to your words gives others the permission to do the same. Avoid sending mixed messages — for example, holding others accountable for getting reports done on time, and then consistently sending out information late yourself. Make sure your behaviours and your words are congruent.

When it comes to addressing tough stuff, hold a mirror up to your own behaviours and make sure you're demonstrating the changes you want to see in others.

Dealing with the tough stuff can provide the fertile ground for deeper connections, innovative strategies and greater commitment to a cause. And we believe these are all worth pursuing to establish better relationship economies.

In rapidly changing times there's one other economy we need to explore that's critical not only in strengthening our relationships, but also in dealing with the tough stuff.

The confidence economy

For years now the world has known that change is the only constant that we can rely on in the workplace. We've all been through downsizing, upsizing, restructuring, decentralising, multiskilling, specialising and amalgamating. But the change currently taking place in the business world is monumental. The level of uncertainty in the financial, business and housing markets is high, and uncertainty is infiltrating many of our conversations.

So how do we navigate this new landscape of constant uncertainty and rapid change? The reality is that people buy confidence in uncertain times. In an uncertain marketplace, confidence is the currency people trade in. So now is the time to not only get good at what you do, but also to get great at it and ooze confidence. Then match every part of what you do to this newfound level of confidence.

Invest time and energy into selling confidence not only through your message and your expertise, but also through the quality of your processes, products and materials. Make sure you interact with and engage customers with confidence and care. In connecting with your team and work colleagues, ensure your message is not, 'We will get through this', but rather, 'We will excel through this'. Everything about your business, about your presentation and about how you interact and engage with customers and employees needs to ooze confidence in these turbulent times. Positive reinforcement is the key to having this confidence extend past your own actions and to the actions of others.

Engaging in positive reinforcement with others is brain changing. The simple act of saying 'thank you' and encouraging the specific behaviours that you want from others at work will strengthen the neural pathways in their brain. The neural pathways are intricate webs of connections that are constantly evolving, growing, weaving, connecting and disconnecting with other pathways, forming something like a matted web of tree roots. In his book *Quiet Leadership*, organisational coach David Rock suggests that hearing the encouraging sounds of positive reinforcement helps our brains to know which connections to preserve and strengthen and which to prune. Which pathways grow and become stronger in our brain and which ones fade away depends on the amount and type of attention that is given to that link. He goes on to say, 'Neurons literally need positive feedback in some form to create long-term connections. If we want to help people improve their performance at work, we need to become much more proficient at giving positive feedback'.

You may have heard the saying, 'We are what we repeatedly do'. This could be adapted to, 'We are what we are repeatedly reinforced and encouraged to do'. What is unique to each individual is that what reinforces one person may be quite different from what reinforces someone else. Getting to know the individuals at work and their main reinforcers will help you target your interactions with them for maximum effect.

Dealing with the chuff stuff

It's easy to focus only on the tough stuff when managing people at work, but sometimes we forget the chuff stuff! The problem in giving attention only to the negative behaviours is that you risk creating a moderated, average work team.

To have someone achieve excellence they need to hear feedback about what they are doing well: they need to be reinforced. Here's the coolest thing: when you reward someone by expressing gratitude, you effectively reward yourself in the process.

If you do find your ratio of tough stuff to chuff stuff is heavily skewed in favour of the tough stuff, then set yourself the task of finding a reward or reinforcer for a staff member every day for a week, or twice a week for a month. Remember to vary the timing and size of the reinforcers for best effect (don't let them become predictable), and in turn see the change in people's productivity as a result.

One of our earliest messages in this book was a prescribed, even required, focus on the goodness of people—the notion that all people are awesome. Although we've put an array of tools in front of you throughout the book, don't ever lose sight of the fact that we are wonderful beings, each one of us. There is perfection in our imperfections.

Enjoy the results of your new approach.

INDEX

QUICK QUESTION... WHAT ELSE DO YOU GUYS DO? THOUGHT YOU'D NEVER ASK!

Firstly, thanks for taking the time to soak up this book. It's time for you to get to work and put some of the ideas and insights you've read into practice. It's a worthy quest.

But if you are also keen to drink in more - even get rolling drunk on wonderful workplace thinking - then it's time for us to introduce you to Pragmatic Thinking.

Pragmatic Thinking is a behaviour and motivation strategy company. We work with cage-rattling leaders and adventurous corporates who don't just invest time on their business strategy, but also in getting clear on how they can get people implementing this strategy (that's the real key right?).

We work across three main areas including:

CULTURAL ROAD-MAPPING - have a new culture you need to create but not sure how to get your people there? We're like the ghost-busters in this field, minus the Ray Parker Jnr soundtrack.

LEADERSHIP CAPABILITY - need get the best from your organisation's leadership? We build custom leadership programs based on science to suit your current and future needs. Ultimately, you end up with a 'made' one, not a 'bought' one. They're rad.

FEEDBACK FOCUS - want to make sure it's not just you who has the skills and capabilities to get results from these tough conversations? Bring us on board. If the feedback culture in your business is underperforming, we can turn it around.

We speak and consult globally on these three areas. When we're not hanging out with the best clients in the world, we put out a regular newsletter sharing our latest research and insights. You can subscribe at >>> WWW.PRAGMATICTHINKING.COM <<<

Send us an email if you'd like to chat about any of the above. Happy to help. :-)

Pragmatic Thinking

A BEHAVIOUR & MOTIVATION STRATEGY COMPANY

LEARN MORE AT:
WWW.PRAGMATICTHINKING.COM
AND REACH OUT ON
INFO@PRAGMATICTHINKING.COM

Connect
with WILEY ▶▶▶

WILEY

Browse and purchase the full range of Wiley publications on our official website.

www.wiley.com

Check out the Wiley blog for news, articles and information from Wiley and our authors.

www.wileybizaus.com

Join the conversation on Twitter and keep up to date on the latest news and events in business.

@WileyBizAus

Sign up for Wiley newsletters to learn about our latest publications, upcoming events and conferences, and discounts available to our customers.

www.wiley.com/email

Wiley titles are also produced in e-book formats. Available from all good retailers.

WILEY

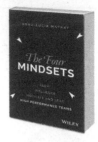